DARE WE SPEAK OF HOPE?

Dare We Speak of Hope?

Searching for a Language of Life
in Faith and Politics

Allan Aubrey Boesak

WILLIAM B. EERDMANS PUBLISHING COMPANY
GRAND RAPIDS, MICHIGAN / CAMBRIDGE, U.K.

Published 2014 by
Wm. B. Eerdmans Publishing Co.
2140 Oak Industrial Drive N.E., Grand Rapids, Michigan 49505 /
P.O. Box 163, Cambridge CB3 9PU U.K.
www.eerdmans.com

Printed in the United States of America

20 19 18 17 16 15 14   7 6 5 4 3 2 1

Library of Congress Cataloging-in-Publication Data

Boesak, Allan Aubrey, 1946-
    Dare we speak of hope?: searching for a language of life in faith and politics /
    Allan Aubrey Boesak.
        pages   cm
    Includes bibliographical references and index.
    ISBN 978-0-8028-7081-0 (pbk.: alk. paper)
    1. Hope — Religious aspects — Christianity — Congresses.
    2. Race relations — Religious aspects — Christianity — Congresses.
    3. Reconciliation — Religious aspects — Christianity — Congresses.
    4. Christianity and politics — Congresses.   I. Title.

BV4638.B54   2014
234'.25 — dc23

                                                    2013038806

Unless indicated otherwise, all Scripture quotations are from the New Revised
Standard Version of the Bible, copyright 1989, Division of Christian Education
of the National Council of Churches of Christ in the United States of America.
Used by permission. All rights reserved.

In memory of

Sarah Helena Boesak

And for

Mama Lois Johnson

Iva Carruthers

and

Elna Boesak

all spiritual sisters of Hope's beautiful daughters.

Contents

Foreword

Many Christians, when they hear the word "hope," think of being delivered from this present evil world when they die and entering heaven. Hope for them is hope for the Age to Come, as they understand that.

Allan Boesak affirms the hope of Christians for the Age to Come; but the hope of which he writes in this book is different. The hope here is the hope for justice in this present age. This is the hope that the prophet Isaiah expressed when he said of the Messiah to come:

> He will bring forth justice to the nations.
> He will not cry or lift up his voice,
>   or make it heard in the street;
> a bruised reed he will not break,
>   and a dimly burning wick he will not quench;
>   he will faithfully bring forth justice.
> He will not grow faint or be crushed
>   until he has established justice in the earth;
>   and the coastlands wait for his teaching.
>
> (Isa. 42:1-4)

Just as many Christians think of hope for the Age to Come and not of hope for justice in this present age when they hear the word, so too do many Christians, when they hear the word "justice," think of criminal justice. They identify justice with passing judgment on wrongdoers.

Boesak has been the victim of unjust punishment; he could write eloquently and incisively about justice and injustice in the criminal justice system. But his subject here is not criminal justice. Criminal justice presupposes a more basic form of justice: it becomes relevant when someone has wronged someone, treated someone unjustly. Criminal justice becomes relevant when there has been a violation of justice. But this implies that criminal justice cannot be the only form of justice; there has to be another, more basic, form of justice, a form whose violation makes criminal justice relevant. Call this other form *primary* justice. Boesak's topic in this book is primary justice. More precisely, his subject is the struggle for the righting of primary *in*-justice and the role of hope in that unavoidably conflictual struggle. In that struggle the question of hope is always on everybody's mind, and in that struggle it's all too easy to lose hope.

Boesak is not writing about this struggle from some perch on high, up above the fray. The location from which he writes is down in the trenches. Boesak was one of the leaders of the anti-apartheid struggle in South Africa, and that experience shapes his discussion, giving it an unusual poignancy, vividness, and concreteness. It is because Boesak writes from the perspective of someone who has been part of the struggle to right injustice that his discussion takes the fresh and innovative form that it does: we can speak of hope, he says, only if we also speak of woundedness, only if we also speak of anger and courage, only if we also speak of struggle, only if we also speak of seeking peace, only if we also speak of fragile faith, only if we also speak of dreaming. One and all, these are essential components of the struggle to right injustice.

This is not, however, the narrative of a resister. Though there is a good deal of narrative in it, this is a theological essay, the theology made tangibly concrete by the fact that a good deal of it consists of Boesak's reflecting theologically on his own experiences as a member and leader of a resistance movement. This is theology *in concreto*. I should add, however, that Boesak is not myopically fixated on the South African experience; he regularly brings into the picture other struggles to right injustice.

What also lends concreteness to the theology is the wealth of biblical exegesis. Boesak is a theologian whose thinking is shaped at least as much, if not more, by careful reading of Scripture as it is by the writings of his fellow theologians. Boesak reads Scripture through the eyes of the downtrodden. Given his experience, how could he not? As a result, I had the sense over and over, while reading the manuscript, of scales falling from my eyes. Above I quoted the passage in which Isaiah says, of the promised Messiah, "He will not cry or lift up his voice, or make it heard in the street; a bruised reed he will not break, and a dimly burning wick he will not quench." I have never known what to make of these words. *Dare We Speak of Hope?* has opened my eyes to what Isaiah surely meant; it has opened my eyes to the meaning of a good many other passages as well. Though Boesak is, by profession, a theologian rather than a biblical scholar, he is, nonetheless, an extraordinarily insightful exegete. His exegesis is informed by wide acquaintance with biblical scholarship, but he is not afraid to challenge the scholars when he thinks they have missed the point.

The pursuit of social justice — and the struggle to right social injustice — almost always involves politics; and politics almost always involves, or should involve, the pursuit of social justice and the struggle for the righting of social injustice. Thus it is that a good deal of this book is about politics. Indeed, it is all about politics — though not *only* about politics. Boesak does not pull his punches when it comes to the present-day politics of South Africa and the United States; he is a bracing and undaunted prophetic critic of current politics in these two countries. But the seaminess, the cowardice, the obeisance to power and money that characterize politics today do not lead Boesak to urge Christians to avoid politics. Politics, he says, "is a vortex of expectations, disillusionments, and bewilderments, but we cannot step away from it or from our commitment to make it work for justice."

Then he adds these words: "Hope holds us captive; we cannot give her up, let go of her hand, lest we become utterly lost. Yet we now know that where she is to be found is not in the places of comfort and safety. . . . Time and time again, it seems, we have to learn the lesson that while our hope has to shape our politics, the center of our hope never lies in politics or politicians. Christians have to look elsewhere if we are to find a hope that is durable, life-affirming, and life-giving. If we are to challenge and change the world, [we must] keep 'looking to Jesus the pioneer and perfecter of our faith'" (p. 176).

To those who engage in the struggle to right injustice, every day often looks like Good Friday. In this eloquent, challenging, and deeply spiritual book, Boesak forcefully reminds us that after Good Friday comes Easter. So we dare speak of hope.

NICHOLAS WOLTERSTORFF

Foreword

Acknowledgments

The seeds for this book were sown when I received an invitation from the general secretary of the Council on World Mission, Rev. Dr. Collin Cowan, and the moderator of the council, Rev. Dr. Prince Dabeela, to present three keynote addresses at CWM's World Assembly, which was held in Pago Pago, American Samoa, in June 2012, on the theme "Hope, the Language of Life." I was intrigued by the theme and the context in which CWM presented it to me in that letter of invitation, and I was encouraged by the lively responses and discussions the addresses engendered at the conference. I am grateful to CWM for this opportunity and particularly to Revs. Collin Cowan and Prince Dabeela for their encouragement.

The invitation to teach at Butler University and Christian Theological Seminary in Indianapolis for the 2012-13 academic year has also afforded me somewhat more space for thinking, writing, and the testing of ideas away from the pressures of public life in South Africa. Thank you.

As always, my family — Elna, Sarah, and Andrea — has been a marvelous source of love and support despite the fact that most of the writing of this book occurred during a period of transition and adaptation for us as a family, as well as a grueling schedule of teaching and speaking that took me across the United States. Their patience and resilience remain amazing, their inspiration to me indescribable, and their love priceless.

ALLAN AUBREY BOESAK
Indianapolis
Advent 2012

A Place Where Hope and History Rhyme

"So often it appears that history teaches only despair; cynicism can seem to sweep all before it, as it did in the old South African governance. But in a new environment, one that takes unflinchingly the full measure of the past, South Africa can become a safe place for idealism, the sort of place and time where hope and history rhyme."

Kader Asmal, Louise Asmal,
and Ronald Suresh Roberts

"Do we participate in the politics of cynicism, or do we participate in the politics of hope?"

Barack Obama, 2004

"Do you not understand that many of your words and actions are leading many South Africans towards cynicism and away from hope? And do you not understand that you

*are setting yourselves up against the arc of history, which
is and will always be bent towards hope?"*

South African Churches, open letter to the
leadership of the African National Congress
(ANC), December 2012

Daring to Speak of Hope

I am not ashamed to admit it: I cried tears of joy. Both times.
We never dreamed that politics could look like this. Since 1994,
two major and profound historical political changes took place
that not only made and changed history but also created something within the human heart we had not experienced for far
too long: a tidal wave of hope, not just *for* our politics but *in* our
politics. That at the heart of it all should be black South Africans and black Americans, people who in so many ways bear
in their bodies the scars of struggle for the sake of all humanity,
and thus the bearers of so much hope for all humanity — "God's
suffering servant for humanity," theologian James Cone calls
them — made that hope more than just romanticized political
hyperbole.[1]

Biblically speaking, these children of slavery and Jim Crow
in the United States and the children of slavery and apartheid
in South Africa feel themselves the "earthen vessels" that the
apostle Paul spoke of. We might have been "afflicted in every
way, but not crushed; perplexed, but not driven to despair; persecuted but not forsaken; struck down, but not destroyed . . ."
(2 Cor. 4:7-9). In that "but" we treasured and protected our
hope, the hidden strength that made us go on every new day,

1. See James H. Cone, *God of the Oppressed*, rev. ed. (Maryknoll, NY:
Orbis, 1997).

Introduction

because carrying the death of Jesus in our bodies, as Paul goes *good*
on to say, also means that we were carrying Jesus' resurrection *line*
in our struggles for life.

In 1994, South Africa's people emerged from centuries of struggle and chose Nelson Rolihlahla Mandela as the first democratically elected president of South Africa; in 2008, Barack Hussein Obama was elected as the first African-American president of the United States. It is possible now, of course, to look back and speak and write dispassionately about these two moments as political, historical events, evaluate their meaning for history in both countries, and weigh their import for politics in the world — disconnected from the sweeping emotions that captured our hearts. But for the masses, black and white, who for the first time perhaps felt that they mattered, these were life-changing, utterly transforming moments.

For black South Africans especially, it marked the end of three and a half centuries of struggle against colonialism, dispossession, despoliation, and racist oppression, and the beginning of a fresh, nonracial, democratic, and meaningful future. Justice would be real. Our humanity would be restored. Our right to joy and wholeness would at last be held sacred. South Africa would be a safe place for idealism and hope. Have both nations at last begun to slay the demons of our racist pasts?

In the United States, Barack Obama could not have been elected — both times — without significant white support. And in South Africa it seemed as if the work and spirit of the nonracial United Democratic Front could now take root, that we would at last honor, in our work, lives, and hearts, Albert Luthuli's dream of our country as "a home for all" as we embrace the Freedom Charter's call: "South Africa belongs to all who live in it, black and white."[2]

2. See Albert Luthuli, *Let My People Go!* (1960) (Cape Town: Tafelberg,

I was there, on that Sunday in February 1994, standing behind him on that balcony in Cape Town, as Nelson Mandela spoke of freedom, forgiveness, and hope. As my family and I watched President-elect Obama making that amazing victory speech in Chicago, seeing the tears roll down Jesse Jackson's cheeks, the cries "Yes, we can!" reverberating around Grant Park and the world, feeling their echo in our own hearts, I thought: *This is what happens if you keep hope alive.*

About Nelson Mandela, we said that this was the moment when change came to South Africa, to make it a place "where hope and history rhyme."[3] About Barack Obama, we said, "Hope elected our first black U.S. president in 2008. . . . Were it not for hope, this moment would never have come."[4] At last, in our lifetime, the politics of hope had found a voice, and a face. It had come in out of the wilderness and found a home among us.

Now, for South Africans almost twenty years down the line — and for Americans after a first Obama term — the contradictions are sometimes simply too painful to bear. South Africans are rightly proud of their progressive constitution, with its unparalleled guarantees for human rights for all. At the same time, we see the obscene gap between the rich and the poor, and we see the disdain with which the promise of hope is treated by those in power.

In the United States, Barack Obama has transformed life for lesbians and gays and has moved to protect health care for mil-

---

2006), p. 229. The text of the Freedom Charter, drafted by a "people's congress" in 1955, can be accessed at: http://www.anc.org.za/show.php?id=72.

3. See Kader Asmal, Louise Asmal, and Ronald Suresh Roberts, *Reconciliation Through Truth: A Reckoning of Apartheid's Criminal Governance* (Cape Town: David Philip, 1999), p. 216.

4. Brad R. Braxton, "Hope in 3-D," in Marvin A. McMickle, ed., *The Audacity of Faith: Christian Leaders Reflect on the Election of Barack Obama* (Valley Forge, PA: Judson Press, 2009), p. 137.

Introduction

lions, and yet, after the 2012 election, a friend said to me: "I am so glad we won, but I wonder whether we will ever get the hope back." One wonders: Will a second term be a second chance and a determined, reclaimed onslaught on the politics of cynicism and casual neglect? In South Africa prophetic Christians speak in somber but prophetic tones to our political establishment and specifically to the African National Congress about the loss of hope in our politics and politicians. It seems as if apartheid's dark immoral shadow has returned to threaten the rainbow nation: "Do you not understand that many of your words and actions are leading many South Africans towards cynicism and away from hope? And do you not understand that you are setting yourselves against the arc of history, which is and will always be bent towards hope?"[5]

For South Africans, justice — social, gender, sexual, and political — so treasured in our constitution, remains painfully elusive in our politics, and our social and economic policy framework has not achieved real economic transformation, wealth distribution, or the eradication of poverty.[6] Our social and economic inequalities are devastating and make us one of the worst offenders in the world. The clashes between the government and poor township communities — and between the government and trade unions — are becoming ever more frequent,

5. "The church speaks . . . for such a time as this," open letter to the African National Congress from the SACC, TEASA, African Enterprise, and Kairos SA, issued on December 2, 2012.

6. See Sarah Mosoeta, *Eating from One Pot* (Johannesburg: Wits University Press, 2011). "What is disconcerting," says Sampie Terreblanche in response to Mosoeta, is that while at first the ANC regarded the poor as the "deserving poor," and therefore as their first priority, "many in the ANC elite are now inclined to regard the poor as the undeserving poor" (Sampie Terreblanche, *Lost in Transformation: South Africa's Search for a New Future Since 1986* [Johannesburg: KMM Review Publishing Company, 2012], p. 105).

ever more protracted, and ever more violent. For example, the Marikana massacre of August 2012 has redefined not just the character of the ruling African National Congress but in a real sense the character of ongoing struggles for justice.[7]

Perhaps I should explain this a bit more. The mindless killing of the striking miners at the Marikana mine might yet prove to be a turning point for South Africa. Significantly, the churches, in their letter to the ANC quoted above, speak of a "post-Marikana" South Africa. For the churches, the point of reference in terms of what defines our situation is no longer "post-apartheid" but "post-Marikana." And that seems correct to me, even as it is tragic. Just as the Sharpeville massacre in March 1960 finally defined the apartheid regime and simultaneously redefined the struggle against apartheid, so Marikana will redefine both the ANC and the ongoing struggles for justice in South Africa. What the churches see as a moment of historic redefinition lies in this question: What is, at the moment of crisis, the instinctive response of government, and

7. On August 16, 2012, miners at the Marikana platinum mine close to Rustenburg in South Africa's North West Province went on strike for better wages and working and living conditions. In subsequent clashes with the police, thirty-four miners were killed, causing outrage in South African society. The outrage was compounded by disbelief when the National Prosecuting Authority used an old apartheid law, apparently never repealed, the so-called "Common Purpose Law," to arrest 270 miners for murder. The prosecuting attorney viewed the killing of two policemen during the clashes as the real "common purpose" of the strike. By October 2012, strikes were raging across the country: 30,000 workers at Anglo-American Platinum; 15,000 at Goldfields KDC East and West; 9,000 at Goldfields Beatrix Mine in the Free State; 35,000 at Anglo Gold Ashanti; and thousands of transport workers went on strike as well. This was followed by strikes and violent clashes between agricultural workers and the authorities in the Western Cape. Workers had lost R480 billion between 2000 and 2010. See DLF News: www.democraticleft.za.net (accessed Sept. 30, 2012).

how does that response reflect and define the *character* of the ANC government?

The initial and instinctive response of the ANC is not to react as what it claims to be, the people's liberation movement, with its natural bent toward justice for the poor and powerless. From the response of the South African police to the official response of government, to the actions of the National Prosecuting Authority (NPA), the ANC did nothing so much as remind us disturbingly of the old apartheid regime. Its instinctive reaction was not on behalf of the workers, whom it claims to represent, but rather on behalf of the mine owners, whom in fact it now represents. Its instinctive response was not to protect the workers, but to justify unjustifiable police brutality. Its instinctive reaction was not to respond to workers' rights, to join them in their quest for better wages, working and living conditions, securing better lives for themselves and a better future for their children. Rather, its reaction was to protect the profits of the wealthy mine owners. The fact that those mines are now jointly owned by black people — members of the privileged elite, the political aristocracy in whose patronage the ANC now sees its well-being — underscores this point.

In its turn, the first response of the NPA was to fall back on an old apartheid-era law, perverse even under apartheid's illegitimate legal systems: arrest the workers for their "common purpose" of attacking and killing the police rather than immediately instituting an independent inquiry into the causes of the conflict, the almost knee-jerk violent reaction of the police, steeped in its oft-condemned "shoot-to-kill" culture, and how it came about that police fired with live ammunition and succeeded in killing thirteen workers in the first few minutes. Those are the telling, revealing, and utterly shocking features of this event. But it demonstrated precisely the logic of the choices the ANC has made since 1992: its uncritical embrace of neoliberal capitalism, its creation and protection of a small, extremely wealthy black elite whose natural allies are no longer the poor, who sacrificed in the long struggle to rid the country of its racist past, but the upper crusts of white economic power, who are now benefiting in "free South Africa" as much as they did in apartheid South Africa. It is a deadly logic. The historic watershed for us all is not so much in the killings – shocking and revolting as they were. It is in the merciless exposure of what was once a people's movement – the vessel of oppressed people's dreams, hopes, and aspirations.

In capturing this era as the "post-Marikana" era, the churches have discerned, for the second time, a moment of crisis, or a *kairos* – a moment of prophetic discernment, of prophetic truth-telling, of prophetic action. As in 1985, in the midst of that crisis wreaked on us by apartheid, we are now again called to see, to judge, and to act. The scales have fallen from our eyes. We are now called to understand that the issue is not that power is now in the hands of "our" people and that we can thus afford to be complacent. The question now is, as it always is: No matter *who* is in power, do those in power serve justice, dignity, and humanity? Do they bring hope to the hopeless?

Our reconciliation process is stuttering, not bringing the radical justice and reconciliation that it must and that the oppressed deserve. Instead, it is playing handmaiden to the cynical processes of "Realpolitik," which dictate the nature of our democracy. For the vast majority of our people, the words of that fiery nineteenth-century African-American Presbyterian preacher Henry Highland Garner are proving only too true: there are pharaohs "on both sides of those blood-red waters."[8]

8. Quoted in Gayraud S. Wilmore, *Black Religion and Black Radicalism: An Interpretation of the Religious History of African Americans* (Maryknoll, NY: Orbis, 1973), p. 120.

In South Africa, the ruling elite have done — so soon after liberation — precisely what in Deuteronomy the king is exhorted not to do. At the heart of Yahweh's exhortations, and as the first of the "don'ts," Yahweh says: "[The king] must not acquire many horses for himself, or return the people to Egypt . . . since the LORD has said, 'You must never return that way again'" (Deut. 17:16). Horses were instruments of war. Linking that with "Egypt" meant imitating Egypt as superpower, depending on and glorifying war as means of survival, of superiority over other nations, as token of esteem and "greatness." As a consequence, it meant aping "superpower greatness," yet paradoxically placing Israel at Egypt's mercy and therefore at its beck and call, buying into the skewed and perverted logic of superpower politics, accepting for itself their definition of security, adopting for itself their notion of what makes a nation "great," putting the people back into an Egypt mindset.[9] That is the same as denying the people hope, because you have set yourself against the arc of history, which is always bent toward hope, as the churches wrote to the ANC government.

In biblical Israel, the token of greatness was not superiority in war and domination. It was the imitation of the power of Yahweh: liberation from slavery; steadfast mercy and love; and justice done to the vulnerable, the widow, the stranger, and the orphan. Indeed, Israel's very greatness was in the presence of faithful prophetic witness. When Elijah is taken up into heaven on that "chariot of fire and horses of fire" ascending into the whirlwind, Elisha cries out, "My father! My father! The chariots of Israel and its horsemen!" (2 Kings 2:12) What Elisha means to say is, Israel's "weapons" were not chariots and horses and horsemen with their bows and swords and spears,

9. See Allan Boesak, *The Tenderness of Conscience: African Renaissance and the Spirituality of Politics* (Stellenbosch: Sun Press, 2005), pp. 228-29.

but rather the faithful, courageous prophetic presence personified by Elijah. Not military strength, but prophetic power. "Taking the people back to Egypt" can only mean taking them back to the imitation of the superpower, to the state of mindless enslavement, to before the liberation, away from the prophetic presence, to the other side of those "blood-red waters."

In the United States in 2014, the poor are not only a "permanent underclass"; they are an *unmentioned, unremembered underclass*.[10] In the 2012 election campaign speeches that I listened to, I was amazed that the poor were hardly ever mentioned. It is almost as though acknowledging the crippling poverty of millions is too embarrassing for a nation so rich and powerful. But the United Nations Children's Fund (UNICEF), in its most recent report, reveals that the United States has the second highest rate of childhood poverty in the developed world – better only than impoverished Romania.[11] It seems that mentioning the poor would destroy the myth of the American dream and "the greatest democracy in the world." And because the poor are not mentioned, the word "justice" is not mentioned either. Meanwhile, the criminal justice system is now the "new Jim Crow," and the life span of the average young black man in the inner cities is as long as that of a peasant in Bangladesh.[12]

10. See Frank A. Thomas, *American Dream 2.0: A Christian Way Out of the Great Recession* (Nashville: Abingdon, 2012), p. xii.

11. See *International Business Times*, "US Has Second-Highest Rate of Childhood Poverty in Developed World, Only Romania Is Worse," http://www.ibtimes.com/us-has-second-highest-rate-childhood-poverty -developed-world- . . . (accessed Nov. 20, 2012); UNICEF: http://www.unicef. org. The latter concludes that nations with comprehensive government programs designed to protect vulnerable children had the lowest rates of child poverty and deprivation. Contrast this with U.S. military spending, which is on the order of $664.84 billion: http://en.wikipedia.org/wiki/Military _budget_of_the_United_States (accessed Nov. 20, 2012).

12. For life expectancy comparisons, see Christopher J. Murray, San-

As we look on from the rest of the world, and especially the global South, we ponder with much pain why there was no condemnation of torture, why Guantanamo Bay remained open and in use, why there is no word on mass incarceration; why the Palestinians still are never mentioned in the same breath with justice, humanity, and security; why there were more drone attacks on Pakistan, Afghanistan, and Yemen in Mr. Obama's first term than in George Bush's eight years in office, with civilians – men, women, and children – making up most of those killed.[13] And speaking as South Africans who have not long ago emerged from the horrors of the apartheid era, we are stunned to see the United States adopt, and President Obama sign into law, the very laws that became so characteristic of apartheid's fascist state, laws that we fought so hard against: suppression without a proper hearing and indefinite detention without trial.[14]

Sometimes, as in the case of both President Obama and President Mandela, it is said that the real problem is that the people's expectations are simply too high, too unrealistic for the realities of politics. Somehow that makes the disappointments the people's fault, the result of their unsophisticated politics, their lack of understanding that the election of one person – even one

---

deep Kulkarni, and Majid Ezzati, "Eight Americas: New Perspectives on U.S. Health Disparities," *American Journal of Preventive Medicine* 29, no. 5, Suppl. 1 (2005): 6. The phrase "new Jim Crow" is from Michelle Alexander, *The New Jim Crow: Mass Incarceration in the Age of Colorblindness* (New York: New Press, 2010). Both of the above are cited in Allan Aubrey Boesak and Curtiss Paul DeYoung, *Radical Reconciliation: Beyond Political Pietism and Christian Quietism* (Maryknoll, NY: Orbis, 2012), p. 157; see also p. 182, n. 14.

13. See the editorial entitled "From Shoes to Underpants," *The Economist*, December 30, 2010.

14. See "National Defense Authorization Act for Fiscal year 2012": http://en.wikipedia.org/wiki/National_Defense_Authorization_Act_for_Fiscal _Year_2012 (accessed Nov. 20, 2012).

black person — cannot change things overnight. In all honesty, though, it is not the people's fault. More than creating expectations, they responded to expectations created for them. In South Africa, Nelson Mandela aroused our sense of wonder with his passionate words about a reconciliation that would bring justice and make South Africa "a nation at peace with itself."[15] And it was Mr. Obama himself who repeatedly promised meaningful change to a nation desperately in need of change after eight years of disastrous rule, who raised the critical contrast between the politics of cynicism, the politics of ignorance, and the politics of hope.[16] And just so there is no misunderstanding, he writes and speaks as he is reaching deep into the innermost emotional wells of his people, setting himself apart from, and over against, cynicism and blind optimism as "willful ignorance":

> I am not talking about blind optimism here, [that] almost willful ignorance. . . . I'm talking about something more substantial. It is the hope of slaves sitting around the fire singing freedom songs. The hope of immigrants setting out for distant shores. Hope in the face of difficulty. Hope in the face of uncertainty. The audacity of hope! In the end, that is the greatest gift to us. . . .[17]

It is Mr. Obama who urges the American people not to be deceived by blind optimism, not to succumb to willful ignorance, and to reach higher — to something "more substantial." And

15. In his address in the special session of Parliament, receiving the report of the Truth and Reconciliation Commission, February 25, 1999.

16. See Barack Obama, *Dreams from My Father: A Story of Race and Inheritance* (New York: Three Rivers Press, 2004), pp. 445-53. The 2004 edition includes his keynote address to the Democratic National Convention in 2004, from which the second epigraph for this chapter is taken.

17. Obama, *Dreams*, p. 452.

then he speaks those weighty words: the "audacity of hope." The millions who heard him believed him: "Yes, we can!" And indeed they can! To a people deprived of the politics of wisdom and compassion, but devoured by the politics of greed and ignorance, these are words of life. In holding up the possibility of the politics of hope in words and with a passion this generation had not heard before, the people are touched at the innermost core of vulnerability, need, and righteous longing. Then, when politics fail them, they are blamed. That takes hope to a very different place: out of the language of life to within the texts of terror.[18]

Therefore, in light of these political realities and in the midst of growing human pain, we must ask what it means to believe in hope. Where do we go with our woundedness? Have we, like the politicians and the media, spoken too carelessly of hope? Do we have to learn that hope is only useful in politics after having been strained through the sieve of cynicism and expediency? Is it possible for us to walk away from hope, as politics and the media do now — because the hopeful politics of Nelson Mandela and Barack Obama is now no more than a failed political experiment? Will we fall prey to the lure of what Martin Luther King Jr. defined as "detachment": "Too unconcerned to love and too passionless to hate, too detached to be selfish and too lifeless to be unselfish, too indifferent to experience joy and too cold to experience sorrow," we are neither dead nor alive; we merely exist.[19] Are we to disavow Hope's presence, her pull and her power, because "experience" has taught that it is after all too "mushy" for the "real" world?

We must also ask if we will be able to restore faith and hope

18. This now well-known expression is from Phyllis Trible, *Texts of Terror: Literary-Feminist Readings of Biblical Narratives*, Overtures to Biblical Theology series (Philadelphia: Fortress Press, 1984).

19. See Martin Luther King Jr., "Shattered Dreams," in *Strength to Love* (Philadelphia: Fortress Press, 1963), p. 89.

to our politics, if we are not to run away from it. This we know: the poor and the powerless cannot ever let go of hope; that luxury is for the rich and powerful. But we shall have to learn how to find her anew, and recognize her amidst the detritus of our dreams. The struggle continues: How do we reclaim the wholeness of our soul, and make not just South Africa or the United States, but the world we live in, the kind of place where hope and history rhyme?[20] For our world to become such a place, there are vital decisions that we have to make.

Hope and the Significance of Decision

"Things do exist," said that intrepid theologian of the German resistance against Hitler, Dietrich Bonhoeffer, "that are worth standing up for without compromise. To me it seems that peace and justice are such things." But then he added something that made his declaration unique – and Christian: ". . . as is Christ himself."[21] When Bonhoeffer says, "No compromise," I do not understand him to mean a single-minded, ideological dedication to justice and peace. "Standing up without compromise" is not because of one's ideological bullheadedness or one's stubborn self-righteousness, but because of one's faith in and commitment to Jesus Christ. It is in the understanding that justice and peace is the cause of Christ. Or to express it simply: if one says Jesus, one also has to say justice. If one believes in Jesus Christ, there can be no compromise on one's commitment to social justice and peace.

20. See Asmal et al., *Reconciliation Through Truth*, p. 216.

21. See Dietrich Bonhoeffer, *London, 1933-1935*, Keith W. Clements, ed., Dietrich Bonhoeffer Works, vol. 13 (Minneapolis: Fortress, 2007), pp. 284-85.

This conviction does not fall out of thin air. It is the logical consequence of the decisions one makes, as Bonhoeffer had to do. Indeed, it is remarkable how significant is the role of decision in the life of this theologian/freedom fighter. I speak of "decision" here not linguistically — that is, as a word — but theologically, as an act of faith, a fundamental and transformative choice with consequences for oneself certainly, but far beyond oneself. It is an act taken not in certitude or pride but in fear and trembling, walking not by sight but by faith. It is an act whose consequences one cannot foresee nor be completely prepared for, but it is nonetheless taken in what one is convinced is obedience to Jesus Christ. The making of such decisions is indispensable for the understanding and nurturing of hope.

It is perhaps true to say that one's understanding of Bonhoeffer's theology depends on the understanding of the role of "decision" in his life.[22] What has been called Bonhoeffer's "year of decision" (1932-1933) became the lens through which to best view his whole life and work. Early on, during his sojourn and work with the German expatriate community in Barcelona, and at the time of the rising tensions under the Franco regime that would lead to the Spanish civil war, Bonhoeffer discovered the singular and life-changing power of decision for the life of the Christian. "The question before us," Bonhoeffer told his congregation in 1928, "is whether in our own day Christ still stands in the place where decisions are being made concerning

22. In his 29-page essay "On the Church Community," Bonhoeffer uses the words "Scheidung" (distinction), "Entscheidung" (decision), and "entscheiden" (to decide) fifty-three times. See Dietrich Bonhoeffer, *Theological Education at Finkenwalde: 1935-1937*, H. Gaylon Barker and Mark Brocker, eds., Dietrich Bonhoeffer Works, vol. 14 (Minneapolis: Fortress, 2013), p. 676; see also Ferdinand Schlingensiepen, *Dietrich Bonhoeffer, 1906-1945: Martyr, Thinker, Man of Resistance* (London: T&T Clark, 2010), pp. 189-90.

the most profound matters we are facing. . . ."[23] (We shall return to this important statement in chapter 3.)

It is important to remember that the desire to find the place where Christ stands — with the least of these — would lead Bonhoeffer to the people and places where he found strife and struggle, resistance and death, but also hope, and in hope joy, and in joy peace, with and within himself. This is where hope always leads us, to the difficult strife-torn places where bruised, wounded, and dejected people struggle for meaningful life and dignity and in that struggle find hope.

For those of us struggling to hold onto hope in challenging, disorienting times, there is much to learn from this man who died on the gallows even as the bombs of the Allied forces could be heard just outside of Berlin. As he sought the place where Christ stands, Bonhoeffer had to face his own decision regarding what the Nazis called "the Jewish question," independent of the decisions or lack of decisions of his own church. His decision was not about *whether* he himself should act, but *how:*

> There are thus three possibilities for action the church can take vis-à-vis the state: *first,* questioning the state as to the legitimate character of its actions, that is, making the state responsible for what it does. *Second* is service to the victims of the state's actions. The church has an unconditional obligation towards the victims of any societal order, even if they do not belong to the Christian community. "Let us work for the good of all. . . ." The church may under no circumstances neglect either of these duties. The *third* possibility is not just

23. Dietrich Bonhoeffer, *Barcelona, Berlin, New York: 1928-1931,* Clifford J. Green, ed., Dietrich Bonhoeffer Works, vol. 10 (Minneapolis: Fortress, 2008), p. 342.

to bind up the wounds of the victims beneath the wheel, but to seize the wheel itself.[24]

That "seizing the wheel itself" was Bonhoeffer's decision to enter the politics of resistance. For him, the politics of discussion and theorizing could no longer suffice. Once he had made his choice, and once he discovered the place where Christ stands, he knew that neutrality was no longer possible. His language becomes the language of resistance and challenge. Because his body was already in the struggle, his heart had to be there also. As he now understood, "in reality, there are no 'neutrals.' They actually belong to the other side." The "other side," of course, was the side of the Nazis:

> The church confesses that it has witnessed the arbitrary use of brutal force, the suffering in body and soul of countless innocent people, that it has witnessed oppression, hatred and murder without raising its voice for the victims and without finding ways of rushing to help them. It has become guilty of the lives of the Weakest and most Defenseless Brothers and Sisters of Jesus Christ.[25]

In all probability, those words sounded harsh and uncompromising to the church to whom they were directed. Perhaps they do so even today, for those seeking a cheap reconciliation, a

---

24. See Dietrich Bonhoeffer, *Berlin: 1932-1933*, Larry L. Rasmussen and Isabel Best, eds., Dietrich Bonhoeffer Works, vol. 12 (Minneapolis: Fortress, 2009), pp. 11-13. For an excellent contextual discussion of this matter, see also Schlingensiepen, *Dietrich Bonhoeffer, 1906-1945*, pp. 126, 313.

25. See Schlingensiepen, *Dietrich Bonhoeffer, 1906-1945*, p. 277. Bonhoeffer deliberately capitalizes the last few words — even the adjectives, which are not usually capitalized in German — to emphasize that these refer to Jesus' brothers and sisters in the flesh, namely, the Jews.

grace that is not costly, a unity bought at the price of the dignity and the lives of the vulnerable and the suffering. But for the discarded and condemned, the victims of the murderous ideology of the Nazis, this was the language of hope, the language of life. This is not the posturing of ideological fanaticism, nor is it the safe neutral ground of political correctness. This is the "no compromise" of one who knows what is at stake, that this is where Christ is to be found, for God values their lives no less than the life of Jesus Christ. As Jesus is precious, so they, God's wounded and dejected children, are precious.

Creating a Politics Worthy of the Human Spirit

In my reflections on the overall theme of this book, I decided to let each chapter be guided, as a kind of leitmotif, by a quotation from African Christians, persons whose faith in Jesus Christ has led them to see the world through different eyes, to discern the signs of the times, to understand what God was calling them to, and to speak and act with prophetic courage and clarity for the sake of the world, for the sake of God's people and God's creation, and for the sake of the God who has called them to speak and act in times of great challenge. Once or twice, I have taken as chapter epigraphs the words of persons not of the Christian community. Their commitment to justice and immortal wisdom, too, are Africa's gift to all her children, as I hope it will be to all who share these reflections.

They have spoken words of wisdom and insight, dared to stand where God stands in the struggles for life and fulfillment on our continent, and because of that dared to hope in the midst of a darkness when no dawn could be promised; in the midst of pain no balm could heal; in the midst of a death that could not abide even the faintest hope of life. They dared to hope and to speak of life. Through them, God spoke hope and life to generations of Africans and to God's people across the world. Perhaps these words will once again come to life and inspire those who dare speak of hope.

I have tried to avoid discussing hope as if it were a systematic theological or esoteric philosophical category, or, thinking of our experiences the past two decades, as a political curiosity. Rather, I have tried to respond to the spirit of challenge that Hope engenders as she lures us away from our places of comfort to the situations in life where Hope both comes to us and into her own, situations where hopelessness and despair challenge hope itself. The question and answer format of the chapters is more than just a rhetorical tool. It is the recognition of the truth that hope challenges and confronts us before it inspires us. It is an invitation to avoid the temptation to wrap Hope up in pious sentimentality that we speak of while keeping ourselves at a safe distance and keeping our hands clean, and to encounter her in solidarity with those engaged in the life-and-death struggles of everyday life. To dare to offer people hope in chaotic situations of pain, suffering, and struggle should never be easy, or cheap. We should be as conscious as the prophet Jeremiah not to shout "Peace! Peace!" where there is no peace.

In writing this book I have discovered, somewhat to my surprise, how natural it is to speak of Hope as female. I certainly did not deliberately set out to do so. No doubt it is because I have been so strongly influenced — and entirely persuaded — by Saint Augustine on this point, and perhaps also because it is so natural for Scripture to speak of both the Spirit of God *(ruach)* and of Wisdom *(hokma* and *sophia)* as female. The first thing we learn from Augustine here is that Hope is a woman — and a mother. This has all kinds of consequences for how one reads this book.

Perhaps it is also because the hidden voices in the biblical story, the silenced voices of pain and suffering, which are simultaneously the voices of subversion and hence of resistance and hope, are so often the voices of women.[26] Maybe it is because in our own South African struggles those voices have been so well and so persistently represented by women. Perhaps it doesn't matter — but once I discovered it, there was no reason to resist. Hope is, in the words of Dietrich Bonhoeffer (whom we shall meet often in these pages), one who teaches her children to be "stubborn and purposeful" in fighting for those things that are life-giving to the earth and to humanity.

Chapter 1 speaks of the connection between Hope and our perplexities and our woundedness as we contemplate the nature of our politics and our calling as people of faith. Chapter 2 follows Augustine as he speaks of Hope's two daughters, and we consider that the language of hope is first of all a language of anger and of courage — and we try to discover what this would mean for us today. In a sense, Augustine's language becomes foundational for our reasoning throughout the whole book: Hope begins with Anger and Courage. Chapter 3 argues that we discover hope only as she comes to life in situations of struggle, and we explore examples from the South African apartheid struggle to lead us through the argument.

Chapter 4 looks at our globalized world and renews questions of war and peace, violence and nonviolence. We discover why the theology of the "just war" has become so attractive to theologians and politicians alike, and we ask again, What is "the way of Jesus of Nazareth"? Chapter 5 argues that Hope is inseparable from and rooted in faith, and we ask whether the "audacity to hope" creates tension between the demands of faith, prophetic truthfulness, and the reality of politics, and if

26. See Allan A. Boesak, *Die Vlug van Gods Verbeelding: Bybelverhale van die Onderkant (The Flight of God's Imagination: Biblical Stories from the Underside)* (Stellenbosch: Sun Press, 2005).

Introduction

so, whether that tension can – or should – be overcome. Chapter 6 explores the relationship between hoping and dreaming and takes a closer look at the story of Joseph in the book of Genesis. The Epilogue is a meditation on hope.

This book is critical of the nature of our politics. It does not argue that people of faith should avoid politics, but that we should strengthen our commitment to the politics of justice, peace, and equity. Christians became involved in politics, writes Argentinian theologian José Miguez Bonino, even though at first it was a strange, new world for us. We became involved because of the growing conviction that this was the call of the gospel. "We must move into that arena, crudely ambiguous and dirty though it may be, to courageously assume our position as believers, and dare to name God, to confess [God] from within the womb of politics, from within the very heart of commitment."[27]

I write this book in the fervent hope that it might help us understand that contradictions and disappointments in politics and politicians should not deter our determination to hope, that the hope that is the ground for our actions in faith and our faith in action will remain and grow, and that persons and communities of faith and all people of goodwill will continue to confront politics with the hope that is within us. If we cannot make it turn around, then at least we must cause it to understand that the audacity of hope is always stronger than, and will outlive, the power of politics. We are hopeful not just for our own sake, but for the sake of the common good. The unforgettable words of Vaclav Havel – dissident, writer, first president of the Czech Republic, and incurable dreamer of hopeful politics for a more hopeful world – resonate powerfully with all of us:

27. José Miguez Bonino, *Toward a Christian Political Ethics* (Philadelphia: Fortress, 1983), p. 8.

The *sine qua non* of a politician is not the ability to lie; he need only be sensitive and know when, what, to whom, and how to say what he has to say. It is not true that a person of principle does not belong in politics; it is enough for his principles to be leavened with patience, deliberation, a sense of proportion, and an understanding of others. It is not true that only the unfeeling cynic, the vain, the brash, and the vulgar can succeed in politics; such people, it is true, are drawn to politics, but, in the end, decorum and good taste will always count for more.[28]

I write, obviously, as a Christian theologian, but I hope these reflections will be useful to many outside my own community.

Lately I have been deeply impressed and moved by the way Parker J. Palmer talks about politics. He speaks of the politics of our time as the politics of the brokenhearted. It is an expression not found in the technical vocabulary of political science, or in the strategic rhetoric of political organizing, Palmer says. Instead, it is the language of human wholeness.[29] There are certain human experiences only the heart can comprehend and only heart-talk can convey. This is the language of hope I am speaking of, and the hope that this book is seeking to convey. It is not writing off politics — or politicians, for that matter. It is, rather, as Palmer's captivating subtitle says, "the courage to create a politics worthy of the human spirit." This is what I have tried to say elsewhere in my argument for a "spirituality of politics," and a "tenderness of conscience."[30] So I agree with Palmer:

28. Vaclav Havel, *Summer Meditations*, trans. Paul Wilson (New York: Alfred A. Knopf, 1992), p. 12.

29. Parker J. Palmer, *Healing the Heart of Democracy: The Courage to Create a Politics Worthy of the Human Spirit* (San Francisco: Jossey-Bass, 2011), p. 6.

30. See Allan Boesak, *The Tenderness of Conscience*, chap. 7.

When *all* of our talk about politics is either technical or strategic, to say nothing of partisan and polarizing, we loosen or sever the human connections on which empathy, accountability, and democracy itself depend. If we cannot talk about politics in the language of the heart — if we cannot be publicly broken, for example, that the wealthiest nation on earth is unable to summon the political will to end childhood hunger at home — how can we create a politics worthy of the human spirit, one that has a chance to serve the common good?[31]

Palmer makes the point that our hearts can be broken in two ways: broken in sadness at the state in which our world finds itself, and broken open, to see and embrace the possibilities of our own healing and the healing of the world in the doing of compassionate justice. In more than one way, our hearts have been broken, and are being broken still, by the hurts of disillusionment and disappointment, the sense that in all of the things that matter, globally and at home, we are not gaining; the pain of discovering that, for the most vulnerable, justice is a strange and unknown land; that, for the excluded and abandoned, Hope is an orphan. In this book, I start with the assertion that Hope is not an orphan, but a mother with children whose very existence stirs within us that courage to create a politics worthy of the human spirit. That is when our hearts are broken open to see and embrace the other as well as our human responsibilities and possibilities. Ultimately, that is what we and our politics should be about.

31. Palmer, *Healing the Heart of Democracy*, pp. 6-7.

CHAPTER ONE

Dare We Speak of Hope?

Only If We Speak of Woundedness

God is the God with the wounded knee.

Ancient belief of the
Khoi-Khoi people of South Africa

*"[Tell them] not to loose ye glory of God in their families,
neighbourhoods, or places where God casts them."*

Francis, black servant woman
in Bristol, England, 1640s

Hope, the Language of Life

There is something intensely fascinating about Hope, about our deep longing for her life-giving presence in our lives. For even in the certain face of death, our first instinct is not to resign to it but to cling to Hope, if not for this life then for the next. To fight for life in the face of death in hopes of surviving the battle is one thing. But to hope is not just to fight the battle to survive; it is to fight the battle beyond survival, to secure life, not for ourselves so much as for others who are not able to fight at all.

Our capacity to hope is truly astonishing; it is something deeply, intimately, uniquely human. It affirms in the most emphatic way our connectedness to the divine; for God, in whose image we are made, cannot be a God of love and mercy, of justice and peace, or of endless compassion and infinite grace if God is not also, in the most emphatic way, a God of hope. That we dare to hope — in Rev. Jeremiah Wright's famous phrase, have the *audacity* to hope — is even more remarkable. It says as much about our woundability as it does about what South Africa's Steve Biko called the "righteousness of our strength."[1]

Moreover, for me the idea that hope teaches us a language — indeed, *is* a language — in which we can articulate our deepest longings for a life of human flourishing and fulfillment both as God's gift and as our right as children of God, that can lift us out of the depths of despair, empower us to find the liberating and hope-giving God, who "makes a way out of no way," as the spiritual says, drawing us into the vast expanse of our wider imaginings of freedom and joy, is singularly inspirational. Language is powerful because it is deliberate and intentional. It can be utterly destructive, and it can be empowering and liberating. Language can indeed create hope out of nothing, can cause hope to flourish, if it is spoken to be life-giving and life-affirming.

But then, it has to be a new language. The old language of our colonized and crippled minds, the language of fear and trepidation, of unbelief and cynicism, of ignorance and resignation, of internalized inferiorities and externalized submissiveness, cannot produce a new language. Hope is the language of life because it exposes the truth about life. It dislodges and

1. Steve Biko, *I Write What I Like: A Selection of His Writings* (Johannesburg: Ravan Press, 2005), pp. 120-37.

replaces not just the language but also the logic of oppression. Therefore, much depends on whether — and how much — the language is our own. However, reflecting on the use and abuse of hope as a concept in religious (and political) life and how often hope is being offered as no more than the opiate of the poor and oppressed, not to uplift and inspire but to silence and suppress, I thought it might be more appropriate and helpful to turn the affirmation into a question. After all, looking at our world through the eyes of the destitute, the powerless, and the hopeless, because of whose suffering — to speak in the language of Bonhoeffer — God suffers at the hands of a hostile world, a straightforward, uncomplicated affirmation of hope as "the language of life" is too easy, too simplistically religious, perhaps even too arrogant, certainly too obvious.[2] For despite much triumphalist sermonizing that bubbles over with joyous certitude, hope is not cheap, not so easily fashioned out of the pliable clay of our endlessly inventive, market-oriented, consumerist religiosity. Hope cannot be branded, marketed, or commodified.

We must resist the media propaganda that is so quick to categorize our hope as naïve, not-of-this-world, and therefore the attitude of dreamers, as if dreaming a better world is childish, unsophisticated, maladjusted, and not be taken seriously by mature adults, people aware of the "realities" of life. That way we will surely be talked into the too easily acquired cynicism that so many seem to thrive on. Contrary to what many might think, cynicism does not make unbelievers of us. Nor does it make independent thinkers of us. Rather, it makes us believers only of "what we can see," that which can be conjured up by the powers of domination, held up us eternal, self-evident truths. It makes us believers in the myths on which those powers depend. Cynicism does not make us more mature; it makes us

2. See chapter 3 below.

foolish and apathetic. There is nothing unreal about injustice, indignity, and oppression, and there is nothing naïve about justice, dignity, and equality and the struggle for a better world.

The sickness eating away at our politics is its alienation from humanness, its fear of a spirituality of politics, its inability to connect with the core of our human-being-ness. Despite our disillusions, this is not the time to run away from our responsibilities, political or otherwise, and in so doing to run into the arms of the myth-makers in the service of the imperial logic. This is the time for the "tremendous decision" we have to make, as Bonhoeffer reminds us he had to make as well:

> This is where a tremendous decision takes place: whether we Christians have enough strength to witness before the world that we are not dreamers with our heads in the clouds . . . that our faith really is not opium that keeps us content with an unjust world. Instead, and *precisely because our minds are set on things above, we are that much more stubborn and purposeful in protesting here on earth.* . . .[3]

This is how Bonhoeffer understands Colossians 3:1-3, the text that exhorts us to set our minds "on the things that are above, not on things that are on earth." For Bonhoeffer this does not mean that we turn our back on the things of the earth. Rather, it means to be faithful to the earth *for the sake of the things that are above.* For Bonhoeffer, the "things of the earth" are not silly indulgences or shallow pleasures. He is thinking of justice, peace, human worthiness, and the search for hope and a meaningful life — the things that would reflect the will of God

---

3. See Ferdinand Schlingensiepen, *Dietrich Bonhoeffer, 1906-1945: Martyr, Thinker, Man of Resistance* (London: T&T Clark International, 2010), pp. 111-12 (italics added).

on earth "as it is in heaven." In truth, though, "to be faithful to the earth for the sake of the things above; to let one's earthly hopes be renewed by eternal hope, dashes any hope for a comfortable life," as the German Bonhoeffer scholar Ferdinand Schlingensiepen interprets this passage, because Bonhoeffer goes on to talk about our readiness to shed our blood in defense of this hope and this action in faith.[4] But that is indeed what it means to stand up for the things of the earth: justice, hope, dignity, redemption, wholeness. Standing for justice and hope is not for the faint-hearted, or for the seekers of a comfortable life, innocent of the risks of faith. The lives of the true prophets, from the ancient faith traditions to those of our own day, offer testimony to that.

The Hope That Does Not Disappoint

Therefore, we must take Paul quite seriously when, in Romans 5:1-5, he puts hope at the end of a process not at all easy or obvious. If we use the alternative and, in my view, better reading of this passage, "let us" (as exhortation) instead of "we have" (as declaration) — as other ancient manuscripts suggest — Paul's meaning becomes even clearer. Then, too, the "boasting" ("to glory in") is not an a priori affirmation that we can take for granted. Neither is it some Christian sociomasochism in which we actually enjoy suffering because of some "glory" martyrdom brings us. Rather, it becomes an invitation. We accept God's invitation; we join God in God's struggle for the liberation and flourishing of all God's creation and all God's children, and only in this way do we "boast in [kouchaomai — rejoice in] our hope of sharing the glory of God."

4. Schlingensiepen, *Dietrich Bonhoeffer*, p. 112.

It is not as if we are entitled to any glory, or perversely revel in our pain, but that rejoicing comes as a result of our acceptance of the invitation of what follows: "Let us glory in our hope," Paul then says, but "let us also glory in our sufferings." Then it becomes a rejoicing that counts, knows, and bears the costs. We are ready to face the costs of the suffering we know the enemy will inflict, because our courage is anchored in our faith in God and our peace with God. I did not understand this text properly until I was in the thick of the struggle, facing dogs and guns and tear gas; marching with the incredibly brave youth of South Africa, who were sharing their courage and hope with the rest of us; and having to deal with threats to my life and with the fear from within my own heart.

No, it begins with "our sufferings," knowing that suffering always comes with any struggle for the things that matter. It "produces endurance, and endurance produces character, and character produces hope," which is the Hope that "does not disappoint," that does not put us to shame. Those who find Hope will find her through suffering and endurance. Those who seek a shortcut, avoiding that long, uphill battle of endurance, will only conjure up a mirage, a hope that disappoints.

real hope comes thru struggle

Francis — we do not know her real name, nor where she came from, only that she was brought to England against her will — was a "blackamoor," a woman who lived as a servant, the poorest of the poor, amongst "the hewers of wood and the drawers of water" in Bristol, England.[5] Lying on her deathbed in the 1640s, she sent a message to "all of the assembly," her Christian worshiping community, including servants like her, the poor and destitute, and those held in the chains of slavery. "Tell

5. See Peter Linebaugh and Marcus Rediker, *The Many-Headed Hydra: Sailors, Slaves and Commoners, and the Hidden History of the Revolutionary Atlantic* (Boston: Beacon Press, 2000).

them," she said, "not to loose ye glory of God in their families, neighbourhoods, or places where God casts them." She sent this word to those who, like her, believed that there is a struggle to be fought for justice, whose end was

> that we may work in righteousness, and lay the foundation of making the earth a common treasure for all, both rich and poor. That everyone that is born in the land may be fed by the earth . . . not one lording it over the other. . . . So that our Maker may be glorified in the work of [God's] own hands, and that everyone may see [God] is no respecter of persons but equally loves [God's] whole creation. . . .[6]

Francis's exhortation is "not to lose the glory of God," not just in the comfortable places – families and neighborhoods – where it is easy to hold on to that glory, where others believed like they themselves did, where there were shared commitments, shared burdens, and shared struggles, and hence shared solidarity and encouragement. She speaks of those places "wherever God casts them." Those would be the places of strife and contestation, those places they would rather avoid if they could, the places of challenge, suffering, despair, and of utter abandonment. She speaks of the wilderness places where Hagar, hopelessly lost, would dwell with her helpless child, where fear and desperation are one's constant companions. The place where Elijah would curl himself under a bush and cry out for death, because he thought that what he did for the glory of God was in vain. The places from

6. Linebaugh and Rediker, *The Many-Headed Hydra*, p. 73, where they cite the Digger Manifesto from 1649, a document of the "Diggers and Ranters," a group working for social justice and whose beliefs were held in common with the "assemblies" that Francis belonged to – hence her specific reference to "glory."

which Jesus would beg for the cup to be taken away from him and from which he would scream the anguish of his abandonment to the heavens.

What does Francis mean when she says that they should not "lose the glory of God"? Perhaps the insights of this child of Africa can help us understand this better. First of all, I think that "to lose" here does not mean in the first instance to think of the glory "getting lost," as if by some accident, or by the vagaries of life. To "lose" here means "to let go," as a choice we make, a deliberate act on our part. Francis was a slave; she knew that the lives of slaves would always be a struggle for freedom and justice, for dignity and meaning. In that struggle was not just their survival, perhaps their salvation, but also the glory of God. It would be hard: through the course of it all, their lives would not be worth a cent. The temptation to let go, to seek an easier path, to hide in the safety of resignation and submission, is always great, so great that it is disorienting. Every enslaved person knows that. Losing the way is losing the glory. So she cautions against the easy way, because that would not only mean giving up on the struggle for meaningful life, it would be letting go of the glory of God.

Secondly, "to lose" could also mean that the glory could be forcibly taken away by those who would rather keep the world the way it is, those who benefit from the oppression, suffering, and exploitation of the subjugated. Francis understood that the powerful never give up their power and privilege without a struggle. In taking away the dignity of the oppressed, in depriving them of even the desire for freedom and justice, they would deprive them of the glory of God. Holding on to the glory involves resistance, and resistance brings suffering. She is blessing them with strength and righteousness and endurance. She is not uttering pieties on her deathbed; she is spurring on to action. Her words are not the farewell mumblings of a drifting mind; they are the enabling, empowering language of hope and life.

But what does she mean by this "glory"? It is not the glory of majestic, resplendent, beautiful buildings that she means. Neither is it the glory of the reveling in our own self-aggrandizement. For Francis, Linebaugh and Rediker write,

> Glory signified the transcendental present — not a *passive* waiting for a future in Heaven, but *actions* to be taken by the dispossessed, to create Heaven here on Earth. Glory appeared through devout expression that mediated between holy text and subjective experience. It might sound like groaning, howling, screeching or screams of pain, but it had the power to transform persons. . . . The discourse of glory among the humble assemblies of the 1640s was synonymous with audacity and originality.[7]

Even today, this is what the shouts of "glory!" in the black church mean when shouted in response to the realities of pain and struggle. We do not glorify suffering, but we rejoice in the fact that we might be part of that struggle even if it causes us pain and suffering, because it is the road to victory. "Nobody knows de trouble I've seen," sang the African slaves. "Glory, Hallelujah! Sometimes I'm up, sometimes I'm down; sometimes I'm almost to the ground; Oh Yes, Lord! Glory, Hallelujah!" This is the glory we "share with God," because it is this very God, says the sixteenth-century reformer John Calvin, who has planted within us that longing for justice, peace, and human fulfillment. Calvin, when speaking of the cries of the poor and the oppressed, goes on to say that when they, like the psalmist, cry "How long?" "it is then as

---

7. Linebaugh and Rediker, *The Many-Headed Hydra*, pp. 83-84 (italics added).

Dare We Speak of Hope?

though God *hear[s] himself,* when he hears the cries and groaning of those who cannot bear injustice."[8]

Moreover, the "boasting" Paul talks about is so steeped in our "justification by faith," so marked by the "access we have through Jesus Christ," so soaked in the "grace in which we stand," that we are cautioned almost at once not to take this "boasting" in the sense that we usually understand it. It is better to understand it as "speaking boldly," which is further qualified by the "hope" of sharing the glory of God. Nothing is taken for granted here. No wonder faith, hope, and conviction are so intimately connected in the Bible. Faith is truly "the assurance of things hoped for, the conviction of things not seen" (Heb. 11:1). Conviction, without the hope in the things not yet seen, is not faith — it's just arrogant certitude. We are confident, not in ourselves, but with the confidence Paul calls upon three chapters later, where he is "convinced" about the surety of God's love for us in Christ Jesus (Rom. 8:38).

So it seems proper that we, while not letting go of the affirmation, let the affirmation be shaped — be given "character," if you will — by raising the humble, and humbling, and perhaps the troubling question: "Dare we speak of hope?"

The language of hope begins, as it always must, with a question. The "Dare we even speak of hope?" question triggers other questions: Who speaks of hope? To whom do we speak of hope? How shall we speak of hope? And just as important, shall we allow Hope to speak for herself? Shall we allow Hope to speak to us, so that in listening we may learn to speak differently? When Hope has taught us to speak, shall we then speak her language without fear, challenging the language of meaningless religiosity, patriotic uniformity, and political conformity? For if there

8. John Calvin, *Commentaries on the Twelve Minor Prophets,* vol. 4: *Habakkuk, Zephaniah, Haggai* (Grand Rapids: Eerdmans, 1950), pp. 93-94 (italics added).

is one thing that we have learned through our struggles and our faith, it is that the language of hope is first the language of suffering and pain; of truth and anger and courage; of protest and confrontation and endurance – before it is the language of comfort, uplifting, and joy. It screams before it soothes. The language of hope is a language that scorches the tongue of the powerful, the arrogant, and the violent. In the mouths of the deceitful, the comfortable, and the complacent, it grits like sand between the teeth. On the lips of the faithful it is a balm. Speaking of hope should disturb us before it comforts us.

The God with the Wounded Knee

Little by little, we are beginning to understand more and more about the first nations who lived in the southern parts of Africa when the white colonists came, the Khoi and the San peoples, their way of life, their culture, and their ancient religion. One of the pillars of this ancient faith was the belief in a supreme being, the Giver of all good things, the Protector and Sustainer of all creation. Another pillar was the awareness of their oneness with the earth, their dependence on and resonance with nature. A third was their awareness of the truth that their very human-being-ness depended on the life-giving interrelationships with other human beings. This is what preserved their wholeness as human beings; this is what made them "Khoi-Khoi" (note the repetition): people amongst, for, and because of other people. Their name was not a geographical designation; nor was it an ethnic identification. The very name was their placement amongst humanity.

They called their god Tsui//Goab.[9] From Tsui//Goab comes

9. In the written Khoi language, the slashes represent the different

the rain, the food in the earth, the wild animals in the fields, indeed all of life itself. From Tsui//Goab also comes the gift to live humanly with each other, the gift that makes us understand the fragile, and thus precious, bonds between humans, and humans' bonds with the earth we live on and share with each other and the rest of creation — hence their name, Khoi-Khoi. Their very existence depends on how they live as humans with and among other humans, and with nature. Our interdependence is life itself, they say: we sustain each other as nature sustains us.

When they die, they are buried in a sitting position, facing East, where Tsui//Goab, living in the Red Light, arises to give new life to every new day. That light is the announcement that as God comes to take those who have died, God affirms new life to all — every day. Returning to the earth is not to cease to be; it is to be taken up in other, eternal cycles of life. So the earth is not a deathbed; it is a gateway. It is not a fearsome thing, for the earth is not an alien place, nor hostile ground. She is a mother to whom we return.

What about evil then? For the Khoi-Khoi, //Gauab is the Evil One. //Gauab is the enemy of God and the enemy of all that lives, the destroyer, the one who sends the storms, famine, and

---

clicks that are characteristic of the language of the Khoi, San, and Nama peoples. It is the click in all its different forms that isiXhosa assimilated through the interaction and intermarriage of the Xhosa with the Khoi in the Eastern Cape early on. Already that makes isiXhosa very distinctive from the other Nguni languages, such as isiZulu (whose clicks are softer) and Setswana or Sesotho and other "Northern" South African languages, which have no clicks at all. In this case the click indicates that it should be combined with Goab. For the ancient beliefs of the Khoi-Khoi, see Theophilus Hahn, *Tsuni//Goam: The Supreme Being of the Khoi-Khoi* (London: Juta, 1881); see also Willa Boezak, *So Glo Ons! Die Khoe-San van Suid Afrika* (Kimberley: Northern Cape Provincial Ministry for Environmental Affairs and Tourism, 2007), pp. 28ff.

illness. //Gauab is the origin of ill will, of the evil humans do to each other. From //Gauab come our pain and disappointments and bewilderments. //Gauab is the supreme exploiter of our weaknesses and fears. In the languages of the Khoi and San, says Willa Boezak, words such as "misery," "destruction," and "annihilation" all have their roots in the word //Gauab.[10]

Tsui//Goab and //Gauab, the Khoi believe, have been in constant battle for a long time. The battle has been intense, the Khoi tell us, because God is not fighting on God's own behalf, but on behalf of God's creation. Tsui//Goab is victorious in the end, but //Gauab takes a long time to die. And as he dies, he continues to destroy as much as he can. So, what about our battles to survive, to overcome evil in all its frightening forms, our daily setbacks and the indescribable hurt we do to each other? All of that is //Gauab's determination to do damage even as he is dying. Our afflictions are but his dying efforts to hurt God's children, even though he knows that the battle is over, and he has lost.

To me, that sounds like an apocalyptic scene from the Bible — something like the battle between Michael and his angels and the dragon. The power of the dragon is fearsome: with his tail he sweeps down to the earth a third of the stars. Even though the dragon is defeated, he still fights and "pursues the woman." When the dragon cannot destroy the woman, he goes after her children, seeking *their* destruction (Rev. 12). In the Khoi legend, Tsui//Goab defeats //Gauab; but the latter continues to pursue God's children, and that battle never ends.

Lest we think of this as just another muscular religious tale, the tale of a just another violent warrior-god, let us consider the following. First, God enters the battle in solidarity with God's creation. Tsui//Goab, after having created the world and all that

10. See Willa Boezak, *So Glo Ons!* p. 28.

good antidote to triumphal God

is in it, simply could have stepped back and "rested." But leaving the creation to itself, letting human beings defend themselves against evil forces in an uneven battle they would surely lose, allowing God's creation to be destroyed – that was unthinkable. Second, and more importantly, though God was victorious, they say, in that ancient and ongoing battle God was wounded in the knee. That is why the supreme being is called Tsui//Goab, which literally means "wounded knee."[11] The supreme being of the Khoi is not an almighty God whose highest attributes are power and omnipotence. Their God is a wounded God.

I think that this means the following: When the Khoi thought of their God, they first thought of *woundedness*; second, they thought of *solidarity*. Tsui//Guab was in the first place not a God of power and might, but of woundedness and empathetic solidarity, a God who fought on behalf of the God's creation and children, and who was willing to be wounded for their sake. They do not see their God imperiously striding the universe "like a colossus"; rather, they see their God limping beside his wounded children, standing between them and destruction. The struggle against evil continues every day, the ancient Khoi say, as creation suffers indescribable assaults, the human capacity for evil takes one's breath away, and the pain of our daily existence stands like //narrabush on the veld. But we know that //Gauab's continued attack on creation and on God's children is an attack on the holiness and worthiness of Tsui//Guab's very being.

good

Because Tsui//Guab is wounded, the ancients go on to say, God understands the woundedness and the woundability of

11. The myth of "Wounded Knee" was first recorded by Th. Hahn in his groundbreaking work on the religion of the Khoi; but I am especially grateful to Willa Boezak, who did considerable research in conversations with still-existing Khoi communities in the Northern Cape, for his insights into and interpretation of this belief. Here I take this interpretation considerably further.

God's creation, of God's children. God understands when we are made vulnerable by powers that seek our destruction. Tsui// Guab knows that we are limping along, struggling to survive, to remain standing in the storm, battling with our frailties, struggling with the assaults on our dignity and our humanity that seek to devour our capacity, our very right, to resist despair. And therein lies our hope: our strength in the ongoing battles against that particular death called hopelessness.

It may well be that this is the answer to the oft-debated question why the Khoi in South Africa so easily opened their hearts to the Christian gospel. It surely cannot be the terrible coercion of the god of the white colonizer, the despoiler and destroyer of all they knew and held dear, and in whose name they were dispossessed, enslaved, massacred, decimated. The lure of the Christian faith could only have been in the fact that they discovered in the crucified Jesus, with the wounds in his hands, feet, and side, so much of the image of Tsui//Goab, the God whose name is "Wounded Knee." In him those ancient Gentiles found their hope.

God Is a Wailing Woman

It is the women who have been persistently more sensitive to this understanding, and have tried to alert us to the dangers, indeed, the utter folly of clinging to the language that speaks of God in imperial, masculine, paternalistic, and warrior terms. Catherine Keller has raised disturbing and profound questions about a theology of omnipotence and how it becomes a temptation that causes human superpower to "ape" divine power. In doing that, however, it "is committing the crassest idolatry."[12]

12. See Catherine Keller, "Omnipotence and Preemption," in David Ray

She is wary of the God of "Job's bewildering whirlwind," a God who becomes "an all-too-human, all-too-masculine, and all-too-imperial idol of power."[13] She is right.

In a solidly reasoned, captivating book, South African feminist theologian Juliana Claassens comes even closer. In wonderfully reimagined imagery, she speaks of God as Mourner, Mother, and Midwife, seeking new ways to speak of God as deliverer.[14] She, too, is searching for a new language, "an alternative way of speaking about God's deliverance that resists the violence and bloodshed associated with this particular metaphor" (p. 7). The metaphor she speaks of is that of God as liberator. In a time when superpowers seek "to devour those that are in their way, a time of a growing sense of the frailty and vulnerability of the human condition," we need to think differently about God, she argues.

The language she seeks is one that leads us away from the worship of an all-powerful, patriarchal, paternalistic God in love with violence to a God whose woundability is more naturally apparent in the ways we speak of – and worship – God. She finds such language in the Bible itself, even though it is not prominent in the familiar texts and is "not [among] the first images to come to mind when we think about God as deliverer." But precisely because these feminine images of God offer the

Griffin, John B. Cobb Jr., Richard A. Falk, and Catherine Keller, eds., *The American Empire and the Commonwealth of God: A Political, Economic, Religious Statement* (Louisville: Westminster John Knox, 2006), p. 131.

13. Keller, "Omnipotence and Preemption," p. 135; see also Catherine Keller, *God and Power: Counter-Apocalyptic Journeys* (Minneapolis: Fortress, 2005), pp. 17-31.

14. Juliana M. Claassens, *Mother, Mourner and Midwife: Reimagining God's Delivering Presence in the Old Testament* (Louisville: Westminster John Knox, 2012). Hereafter, page references to this work appear in parentheses in the text.

Only If We Speak of Woundedness

potential "to speak to people who are dealing with deep-seated experiences of pain . . . trying to survive in a chaotic world where they increasingly have to accept that guarantees do not exist and that things change without warning," a new language about God is necessary (p. 8).

So the liberator-God is not the warrior-God, omnipotent and imperial, but rather the God who appears as a wailing woman, a mother, and midwife, metaphors that offer rich possibilities of an alternative image of God that is rooted "not in death and destruction but in engaged, life-enhancing acts" (p. 7) — in the words of the ancient Khoi-Khoi — "the God with the wounded knee." Claassens appeals to us because, as her point of view comes through her entire book, she looks through the eyes of the exposed and the vulnerable, those who suffer. Perhaps our language about hope could benefit from the language of the ancient Khoi about their God.

Almost intuitively, the Khoi-Khoi spoke of God in this countergrammar, this subversive rhetoric, the need for which is indisputably clear today if we are to speak truthfully, authentically, and hopefully to those "who are vulnerable, those in pain, and those reeling under the effects of unjust power structures . . . [showing] that it is possible to transform a discourse of violence, hatred, and destruction into a discourse of hope, life, and love" (p. 8). It seems clear that learning the language of hope means unlearning the language of arrogant imperialism, which in turn means learning the language of woundedness.

It is a language, I will argue throughout, that is learned only in intense struggles against injustice, oppression, and alienation; against the resignation (and feigned combativeness) of cynicism; against bitterness, hatred, and vengefulness; and against the decay of our souls imprisoned in despair.

Dare We Speak of Hope?

Struggles of Interrupted Hope

Our struggles for justice continue in different ways in new situations and for new generations, and these struggles, I have written elsewhere, are always struggles in hope, and hope is what binds them together.[15] For me personally, the struggle for racial justice evolved into the struggle for socioeconomic justice, for ecological justice, and into gender and sexual justice. The fire that continues to burn in these struggles is the blaze of hope, teaching us that justice is indivisible, as liberation is indivisible. Hope tears the veil of separation between all struggles for justice and opens wide the windows on the world. All these struggles, we have come to understand, are global struggles that bind us — and open us up to — all God's hopeful children in the world. Our concerns can no longer be merely for racial justice in South Africa or the United States, but for the struggles of all God's people, as well as the struggle of the earth as they all join God in God's struggle for justice, truth, restored humanity, and meaningful life.

Hope is the womb in which all these struggles are conceived and nurtured, and out of which they are all born into the world for the healing of the world. For Christians, it is interrupted but resilient hope. Sanctified by the interruption of history by the death and resurrection of Jesus Christ, this hope reveals the violence and injustices at work in the systems of our world and calls for our solidarity with those robbed of hope by the brutal powers of this world, even as it reveals the righteousness of the strength of those who struggle and live in hope. That hope is frequently interrupted by the ruthlessness of the powers of

15. See Allan Aubrey Boesak and Curtiss Paul DeYoung, *Radical Reconciliation: Beyond Political Pietism and Christian Quietism* (Maryknoll, NY: Orbis, 2012), p. 143.

domination and oppression, by the suffering of the people, and it is thwarted by the silencing of the prophets who call for justice. But that hope exposes that interruption and, in turn, works a different kind of interruption: it interrupts the flow of history and the relentless works of evil, turns the world upside down, and shows us to what extent our "reality" is a fake. What is real is the hope that refuses to be broken, ignored, or denigrated — the hope that inspires to action.

That hope is fragile, for it is the hope of the vulnerable, of those at the bottom of the well.[16] But it is resilient, for it is a hope rooted in the promises of God, in the incarnation of Jesus Christ, and in the faithfulness of God's people. "Every new struggle for justice renews that hope; every struggle for justice is renewed by that hope. Every stride toward freedom renews that hope, and every step in dignity is renewed by the audacity to hope."[17] Now, let us begin.

16. The expression is from Derrick Bell, Faces at the Bottom of the Well: The Permanence of Racism (New York: Basic Books, 1992).
17. Boesak and DeYoung, Radical Reconciliation, p. 143.

Dare We Speak of Hope?

CHAPTER TWO

Dare We Speak of Hope?

Only If We Speak of Her Children

"Hope has two beautiful daughters. Their names are Anger and Courage. Anger at the way things are, and courage to see that they do not remain the same."[1]

Saint Augustine of Hippo

"Fighting for the environment is [standing] for the weak, for the poor, for the lonely, for the fearful, for the ignorant, and for the silent."

Wangari Maathai

1. See Robert McAfee Brown, *Spirituality and Liberation: Overcoming the Great Fallacy* (Philadelphia: Westminster, 1988), p. 136. This expression is widely cited but seems to have come to us via Anselm of Canterbury, who attributes it to Augustine. See also Allan Boesak, *The Tenderness of Conscience: The African Renaissance and the Spirituality of Politics* (Stellenbosch: Sun Press, 2005; Glasgow: Wild Goose Publications, 2007), p. 237.

Hope's Girl Children

When that great African theologian of the fourth and fifth centuries, Saint Augustine, speaks of hope, he speaks with the creative imagination of the African mind.

"Hope," Augustine says, "has two daughters: Anger and Courage." In his wonderful imagery, we observe, he does a radical thing: he personalizes hope. In this formulation, hope is no longer an abstract idea, a philosophical concept, or a religious construct. Neither is it an allegory, a fictional figure that must teach us something about human existence. The Augustine who speaks here is not merely the rhetorical genius who philosophizes about life. This is Augustine the astute and clear-eyed observer of the realities of life, the prophet disturbed about justice and injustice, the one who tells us that "an unjust law is not law at all," and who asks the question: "What is government when justice is lacking? It is none other than a gang of robbers!"[2]

This is not about fiction or rhetorical devices. This is about life. And because it is about life, it is about justice. Hope arises out of the encounter with life, with injustice – and the struggle against it. For that reason Hope becomes a person, her name spelt with a capital *H*. For that reason, too, Augustine warns, Hope has two daughters; not characteristics or attributes, but children. Children are an affirmation of life: they open us up to life, and they are exposed to life. And Hope's two daughters have names, Anger and Courage: "Anger at the way things are," says Augustine, "and courage to see that they do not remain the same." The Anger of Hope means that one refuses to accept something that is wrong, to put up with what is driving one to despair. The Courage of Hope means to have the firm resolve to

2. See Augustine, *On Free Choice of Will*, Book 1, para. 5.

pull oneself to one's feet and to attack injustice, even if one has to pay a price for doing so. This is not some innocuous allegorizing gambit. This is what it means to understand the realities of life, to understand the demand for justice. This is a call to join the struggle for fullness of life.

For Saint Augustine, Hope was not the product of that hypocritical, hand-wringing Christian quietism that so many in the church have acquired and made into a spiritual skill: standing idly by, crying "peace, peace" where there is no peace, while the earth is being ravaged and God's people are being destroyed by greed, selfishness, and rapaciousness. That Christianity, in a perverse understanding of reconciliation, seeks to remain piously neutral while the battles for life and justice and truth are raging across the earth, straining to please the powerful and to pacify the oppressed, and calling it "creating hope." That Christianity turns its back on the suffering we ourselves have caused while mouthing pious phrases, our eyes directed toward heaven, but our feet awash in the blood of the innocent. *such* Nor is hope the result of the Christian triumphalism that is so rampant today, certain of every victory, not because we share in the powerlessness, vulnerability, and suffering – and hence the victory of the cross – but because we have made common cause with the privileged and powerful, wielding our Bibles like weapons of mass destruction against those whom we have made vulnerable.

One of the greatest dangers – and temptations – that the church faces when speaking of hope is to sentimentalize it, to make as if it is some cheap ointment we can put on people's wounds, either not understanding or ignoring the true nature and real causes of their woundedness. We submit to romanticized piousness, which denudes Hope of her radical presence in people's lives, thereby shielding ourselves from Hope's radical demands.

We speak of Hope, but it is not the language of life, merely the affirmation of our own imagined certainties, the sycophantic liturgies in the worship of idols, the false gods who claim the place of God in our hearts and lives, our economics, and our politics. We speak of Hope, but rather than the language of life, it is the sanctification of injustice and suffering. It is the cheap, cold, heartless comfort we proclaim as the will of God, with which we hope to placate God while we silence the poor into deeper hopelessness. We speak of Hope, but rather than the language of life, it is instead the celebration of our covenant with death. We see the suffering of God's children, and we hear the groaning of God's creation, but we are not able to be angry, because we cannot share God's *outrage* at injustice. And we do not have courage because we do not share God's *love* for justice. Hope that lacks anger and courage, Augustine teaches us, is not Hope, because we have bereaved her of her children.

Hope is not barren. She does not stand alone and aloof, a haughty, disconnected figure far above the pain and misery of the world, so that her very solitude is a defensive wall against our longing for her and our hunger for justice. She is not a shimmering mirage in the heat of the desert, unreal and thus unattainable, so that our hope for life becomes a mockery of life. She is not an aimless wanderer in the wilderness whose voice is not heard because it is only the echo of the sounds of our anxious, fear-filled nights. Augustine speaks of her not as fiction, holding her up as a lesson in morality, but as a person, a woman, a mother. We cannot ignore her as if she does not exist, turn our backs on her as though she does not matter, trample upon her as though she has no worth, or abuse her as though there would be no accountability. Hope is real, and Hope is alive. She has children.

It is not we who give Hope her daughters. Her children are like Hagar's child, Ishmael, and the children of the mothers of ancient Israel. They are born against all odds, in situations of hopelessness and powerlessness, the offspring not of men but of faith, of fruitful waiting and hoping against hope. They are born through the powerful intervention of Yahweh, who brings life into barrenness, lifelessness, and futureless-ness — when all hope is gone. Yahweh is the "unmistakable agent . . . the one who can turn barrenness into birth, vexation into praise, isolation into worship," creating "a new historical possibility where none existed."[3] Like Ishmael, and like Jesus, child of Mary, they are born into situations of denial and threat, exposed to the rage of predatory power and pure terror. They are born in our embrace of hope, in our exposure to the demands of hope, in our struggles for justice and peace, in our hopeful search for a future and for fullness of life, as Jesus has promised.

Hope does not have a husband. She does not need one. It is with her as it is with the downtrodden, the distraught, and the marginalized of Israel whom we meet in the book of the prophet Isaiah:

> For your Maker is your husband,
> the LORD of hosts is his name;
> the Holy One of Israel is your Redeemer,
> the God of the whole earth he is called. (Isa. 54:5)[4]

Hope does not need the approval or permission or justification of patriarchal power. Not succumbing to its rules and laws, Hope is free; she does what she does because she is who she is. She is not awed by power. In fact, she shuns that power, drenched as it is

---

3. Walter Brueggemann, *First and Second Samuel*, Interpretation series, James Luther Mays, Patrick D. Miller, and Paul J. Achtemeier, gen. eds. (Louisville: John Knox, 1990), p. 12.

4. All biblical references are to the New Revised Standard Version.

in domination and violence. She sings with Hannah that, when Yahweh is your Rock, the arrogance of the powerful no longer intimidates, for their actions are weighed and judged by God. Hope exults in the truth that "the bows of the mighty are broken, but the feeble gird on strength" (1 Sam. 2:3, 4). Contrary to the thinking dictated by power and the belief in violence as essential to power, Hope knows that one does not prevail by might, and that authentic authority lives by truth. When she speaks, she does not threaten; she simply speaks truth to power: "The LORD! His adversaries shall be shattered. . . . The LORD will judge the ends of the earth . . ." (1 Sam. 2:10).

When we embrace Hope, we embrace her children, for she is inseparable from her children, unthinkable without her children, forlorn, lost, and desolate when divorced from her children. Without her children, she becomes only the screaming desperation of our own bewilderment. But we must take note: her children are girl children, and they are called Anger and Courage. Augustine speaks from a time of unquestioned male dominance, of unchallenged, untrammeled patriarchal power. It was a time when the required and only acceptable female attributes were silence, submission, fearfulness, and veneration of male power, whose attributes in turn were anger expressed in self-justified retribution, courage proved in battle, strength displayed in domination, confidence sought in male hegemony, and pride in the skills of war.

Quite simply — but with consummate skill — Augustine turns these assumptions on their head. Women who show anger? Women possessed of courage? That was unheard of, unseemly, and improper in his time. Augustine's names for Hope's two daughters go against the grain: they challenge and confront patriarchy. It is not the anger of bitterness and retribution that diminishes and destroys; it is not the anger that rises in response to hurt done to oneself and one's pride, the response

Dare We Speak of Hope?

when one's domination is challenged. It is a righteous anger because of injustice done to others, the refusal to meekly accept what is wrong, because it is a wrong done to someone created in the image of God. It is anger against the arrogance of power, against the sinful cowardice of feigned neutrality while benefiting from the fruits of injustice and exploitation. It is anger that refuses to give in to hopelessness and resists what drives us to despair. It is the anger of injured but unbowed dignity.[5]

Anger's sister is a girl child named Courage. She is the hope that is the firm resolve to stand up for those who are weak and vulnerable and exploited by the privileged and the powerful. It is the courage to show that courage does not mean skills of war, clever manipulation, and excellence at violent domination. Her solidarity knows no borders, and she fights against all odds and against all forms of injustice because she understands what is at stake. Here truly the weak are girded up with strength, the powerless become powerful, the humble are lifted up.

It is the courage, in the words of the Belhar Confession of the Uniting Reformed Church in Southern Africa, "to stand where God stands; namely against injustice and with the wronged," the courage to know that "in following Christ the church must witness against the powerful and privileged who selfishly seek their own interests. . . ." It is the courage with which the Belhar Confession closes: "We believe that in obedience to Jesus Christ . . . the church is called to do all these things, even though authorities and human laws might forbid them and punishment and suffering be the consequence."[6] It is the courage that knows

5. For further reflection on "righteous anger" within the context of reconciliation, see Boesak, *Tenderness of Conscience*, chap. 6; see also Allan Aubrey Boesak and Curtiss Paul DeYoung, *Radical Reconciliation: Beyond Political Pietism and Christian Quietism* (Maryknoll, NY: Orbis, 2012), chap. 6.

6. For the full text of the Belhar Confession, see Allan Boesak, "To Stand Where God Stands," *Studia Historiae Ecclesiasticae* 34, no. 1 (July

that obedience to God is above all, that the loyalty to Christ transcends all, and thus it challenges all principalities and powers that seek to claim from us the highest loyalty. So the confession ends with this affirmation: "Jesus is Lord."

The Hope of Discontent

In the letter of invitation to address the CWM Assembly that I received, General Secretary Collin Cowan included some sentences from what he called CWM's "statement of discontent." It is a statement that makes clear CWM's understanding of our current world situation and the responsibility of Christians regarding this state of affairs. Dr. Cowan writes:

> "[It is] our statement of discontent [at the despoliation] under which God's creation groans, and in our defiance never to compromise our sense of participation in Jesus' mission of fullness of life for all creation, God's people are obligated to speak the language of life rooted in our conviction that with God, all things are possible. Hope is that language (of life), the indomitable and audacious conviction that we need not settle for mediocrity or second best."

I propose that we take a closer look at this statement, because I see Augustine's Hope and her daughters imaged in these words. The statement speaks of the "discontent" at what we see, namely the "groaning of God's creation" under the weight of rampant injustice and savage greed. It promises "defiance" and commits

2008): 143-72; and "The Confession of Belhar," World Alliance of Reformed Churches, Semper Reformanda: http://wcrc.ch/belhar-confession/.

Dare We Speak of Hope?

itself "never to compromise our sense of participation in Jesus' mission of fullness of life for all creation."

There is, I think, awareness of the fact that, first, we are part of God's creation — not above it, nor separate from it, but intricately part of it. The crisis of creation is our crisis: in the groaning of creation we hear our own anguish. Second, I discern the awareness that as churches we have indeed compromised ourselves on these matters, sought the safety of neutrality in the face of suffering, ensconcing ourselves in the comfort of our sanctuaries and behind the fig leaves of our assembly resolutions instead of boldly stepping into the breach on behalf of God's threatened creation and God's besieged children. Third, as God's children, we are "obligated" to speak hope into people's lives because we are part of God's creation, sharing in God's creative power and compassionate love and justice. Keeping silent is not an option. We are baptized in the name of Jesus, blessed, set aside, forgiven, empowered by the Holy Spirit, and called to be co-workers of God and agents of God's reconciliation.

This is the language of hope, of prophetic clarity, of anger, and of courage. It is the language that the worldwide family of Reformed churches has spoken in the Accra Confession adopted in 2004, which deals with the reality of empire, economic and social injustice, the destruction of the earth, the threat to God's vulnerable children, and the response of faith.[7]

The times we live in, the Accra Confession argues, are times of great urgency: global economic injustice and ecological destruction. The confession depicts a "scandalous world" of

7. For the full text of the "Accra Confession" see *That All May Have Life in Fullness: World Alliance of Reformed Churches' 24th General Council Proceedings* (Geneva: World Alliance of Reformed Churches, 2005), pp. 153-60. See also *Semper Reformanda*: http://wcrc.ch/accra-confession. Paragraph references to the Accra Confession appear in parentheses within the text.

harsh, utterly shocking, and growing inequalities among and within nations, resource-driven wars, poverty, and disease, in which the most vulnerable victims are women and children. These are times of wanton, profit-driven devastation of the earth and rapacious plundering of her resources, and it is all part of a "crisis directly related to the development of neo-liberal economic globalization" (para. 9). Discerning a moment as a *kairos* moment, a time to discern, speak, and act, is crucial in the public testimony of people of faith.[8]

This unjust global economic system is defended and protected by political and military might, and for the poor it has become a matter of life and death. It is an overwhelming system based on the belief that "unrestrained competition, consumerism, unlimited economic growth and accumulation of wealth is best for the whole world; that ownership of private property has no social obligation; that capital speculation, liberalization and deregulation of the market, privatization of public utilities and natural resources, unrestricted access for foreign investments and imports, lower taxes and the unrestricted movement of capital will achieve wealth for all; social obligations, protection of the poor and weak, trade unions and relationships between people are subordinate to the processes of economic growth and capital accumulation" (para. 9).

This reality represents no less than an ideology that claims

8. See the *Kairos Document*, issued in South Africa in 1985, and the subsequent *Kairos* documents issued in countries across the world, the two most recent being *Kairos Palestine: A Moment of Truth; A Word of Faith, Hope and Love from the Heart of Palestinian Suffering* (2009), and *Call to Action: US Response to the Kairos Palestine Document* (2012). For the South African *Kairos* document, see: en.wikipedia.org/wiki/Kairos_Document. For the *Kairos Palestine* document, see: www.kairospalestine.ps. For the U.S. response to *Kairos Palestine*, see: http://ncronline.org/blogs/road-peace/us-churches-respond-kairos-palestine-document.

Dare We Speak of Hope?

to have no alternative, demanding an endless flow of sacrifices from the poor and from the creation. "It makes the false promise that it can save the world through the creation of wealth and prosperity, claiming sovereignty over life and demanding total allegiance, which amounts to idolatry" (para. 10).

The Accra Confession's "scandalous world" pertains as much to the degradation of the earth and to ecological justice as to the human condition and socioeconomic justice. The idolatrous ideology of greed, the worship of money, and the gospel of consumerism have wreaked havoc on the earth.[9] We still do not understand that the "dominion" entrusted to humankind should not be understood as we currently do, "claiming sovereignty over life," where our power and arrogance make us the final arbiters of the life of the earth and all that live in it, but dominion should be understood as making us servants of life — making our lives connected to all other forms of life on the earth. It is for that reason that Africans, ancient and modern, are so insistent on the "wholeness" of life.[10]

Many in the Western world are beginning to understand that as well. "The time has come," says Rachel Carson, that great activist/intercessor for nature and fighter for ecological justice, "for human beings to admit their kinship with other forms of life. . . . [W]e must never forget the *wholeness* of that relationship."[11] Note

9. See Allan Boesak, Johann Weusmann, and Charles Amjad-Ali, eds., *Dreaming a Different World: Globalisation and Justice for Humanity and the Earth; The Challenge of the Accra Confession for the Churches* (Stellenbosch: The Globalisation Project, 2010).

10. See Allan Boesak, *Farewell to Innocence: A Socio-Ethical Study on Black Theology and Black Power* (Maryknoll, NY: Orbis, 1977), pp. 50-51; on the wholeness of life, see pp. 142-52.

11. Cited in Paul Hawken, *Blessed Unrest: How the Largest Social Movement in History Is Restoring Grace, Justice, and Beauty to the World* (New York: Penguin, 2007), p. 57.

that for Carson, as it should be for all of us, the "wholeness" of this relationship lies in its "kinship." It is not an accidental relationship, nor is it a power-over relationship, but it is kinship. It is not power or dominion that is at work here; it is intimacy. Not only does that help us understand the interrelatedness of life and the connections between struggles for justice, human rights and dignity, and struggles for the life of the earth; it helps us see the necessity of the struggle for ecological justice purely *for the sake of the earth*.[12]

Instead, like the *Nephilim* of Genesis 6, we bestride the earth like giants, acting as if nature is our property, ours to take possession of, denying not only our kinship with nature and all of life, but also denying "God's presence immanent in the world," argues theologian Jürgen Moltmann, and he is correct. This nihilistic destruction of nature, Moltmann declares, is "practiced atheism."[13] Our social lawlessness reproduces itself in lawless dealings with nature. We have destroyed the kinship, and in the long run this one, single earth of ours cannot sustain a divided humanity. And this one living earth will no longer endure a hostile humanity.[14]

Again, it comes back to the way we see ourselves reflecting our idolatrous image of God: as all-powerful, omnipotent humans, imposing our boundless will toward domination, madly satisfying that seemingly endless drive to seize power not just over other weaker human beings but over nature, which we

12. See Hawken, *Blessed Unrest*, p. 59; see also Wangari Maathai's insistence that "fighting for the environment was [standing] for the weak, for the poor, for the lonely, for the fearful, for the ignorant, and for the silent" (Maathai, *Unbowed: One Woman's Story; A Memoir* [London: Arrow Books, 2008], p. 188).

13. See Jürgen Moltmann, *God for a Secular Society: The Public Relevance of Theology* (Minneapolis: Fortress, 1999), pp. 99-105.

14. Cf. Moltmann, *God for a Secular Society*, p. 95.

Dare We Speak of Hope?

have turned into a hostile entity that needs to be overcome and dominated in order to be exploited – so that our perceived needs should be satisfied. It is true not just theologically, but also scientifically: humankind as rulers, determining subjects of knowledge and will, stand over against their world and act as though it is "only through lordship over the earth that human beings can correspond to God – Lord and Owner of the earth."[15]

Reading these realities as the signs of the times, the Accra Confession comes to the conclusion that the world – and hence also the Christian church – is once more faced with the challenge of empire. Our reality is an imperial reality.

The Accra Confession's identification of empire and a global imperial reality caused great tensions among the churches. The Globalization Project of the Uniting Reformed Church in Southern Africa and the Evangelical Reformed Church in Germany, a project working with "the challenge of the Accra Confession for the churches," developed a definition of empire that allowed us to deal head-on with the realities of empire and the challenges Accra has identified:

> We speak of empire, because we discern a coming together of economic, cultural, political and military power in our world today. This is constituted by a reality and a spirit of lordless domination, created by humankind. An all-encompassing global reality serving, protecting and defending the interests of powerful corporations, nations, elites and privileged people, while exploiting creation, imperiously excludes, enslaves and even sacrifices humanity. It is a pervasive spirit of destructive self-interest, even greed – the worship of

15. See Moltman, *God for a Secular Society*, p. 99. Hawken speaks of "biological domination," the idea that business and science have a "mandate" to conquer and exploit nature (*Blessed Unrest*, p. 58).

money, goods and possessions; the gospel of consumerism, proclaimed through powerful propaganda and religiously justified, believed and followed. It is the colonization of consciousness, values and notions of human life by the imperial logic; a spirit of lacking compassionate justice and showing contemptuous disregard for the gifts of creation and the household of life.[16]

What it means is this:

- What we are facing is a "coming together," a coalescing of global forces, pooling their resources and power – economic, political, cultural, and military. It is no longer the marshaling of national assets, arsenals, and governmental powers in defense of the national security state. It is the rallying of global forces, of global economic, political, cultural, and military sources in "defense of democracy," for "the protection of civilization" in an imagined "clash of civilizations," in the name of the "war on terror."
- They have defined their goals as *shared* goals, are experiencing them as a unifying force in themselves, and that goal is global hegemony, domination. The powers are "lordless"; this does not mean an egalitarianism, with no "lords" or "underlings," for that is precisely what they create and maintain, and they demand absolute submission. But these lords are not the Lord Jesus Christ. Indeed, they set themselves up as God in the place of God, and therein lies the idolatry that the Accra Confession identifies.
- It constitutes both a *reality* and a *spirit* of domination. We are dealing with structured injustices at both the local and global level, as well as with the subtle political, cultural,

16. Cf. Boesak et al., *Dreaming a Different World*, p. 2.

and economic pressures to conform. "As the soul of systems, the Powers in their spiritual aspect are everywhere around us," according to the wise New Testament scholar Walter Wink. "Their presence is inescapable. The issue is not whether we 'believe' in them but whether we can learn to identify them in our actual, everyday encounters."[17] It is not just in the destruction of human beings and nature before our very eyes; it is in the very air we breathe. For the identification of these lordless powers, we need a spirit of discernment as much as we need the discernment of the Spirit.

- The empire we face is created by humankind; it is not divinely sanctioned, God-given, or historically determined; it is not irreversible, unchangeable, or unchallengeable, as it is claimed. The language we use, in the way we speak of "the Markets," for example, sets up the deification of the markets as a normal thing, as if they were godlike entities that determine, in and of themselves, the destiny of individuals and nations, masking the truth that "the markets" are in fact determined by the rules set up and manipulated by those who control the global capitalist system. It does another thing: it masks the persistent violence inherent in that manipulation, the destruction it wreaks on whole communities for the sake of profits for the few. There is nothing Godlike about it. We are called instead to discern the anti-Godlike spirit that drives this reality. And because it is anti-God, it is antihuman.

- It is an "all-encompassing reality": it lays claim to every facet of life, and it serves, protects, and relentlessly defends the interests of powerful corporations, nations, elites, priv-

---

17. Walter Wink, *The Powers That Be: Theology for a New Millennium* (New York: Galilee Doubleday, 2001), p. 29.

ileged groups — the beneficiaries of empire — to the detriment of those who are its perpetual victims.

- It does this while, with imperial arrogance, it exploits creation, excluding and enslaving — even sacrificing — humanity *for the sake of* power, privilege, and profits. In doing this, to turn again to Walter Wink, empire creates not only the myth of domination, but also "the myth of redemptive violence." Instead of acknowledging the violence it uses because it needs to for continued domination and exploitation, it "enshrines the belief that violence saves, that war brings peace, that might makes right." Consequently, violence is not only necessary; it is the only thing that "works." "If a god is what one turns to when all else fails, violence certainly functions as a god. It demands from its devotees an absolute obedience-unto-death. . . . It, and not Judaism or Christianity or Islam, is the dominant religion of our society today."[18] The imperial arrogance we are speaking of is not simply a misguided attitude; it is a deliberate, continuous act of violent destruction.
- It is a *pervasive spirit*: it manifests itself everywhere, presents itself as the right, necessary, and natural way to think, to be, and to exist. To think and exist differently would be unnatural, an aberration.
- This pervasive spirit always serves the same ends: the destructiveness of self-interest, greed, the worship of money, goods, and possessions. It is the gospel of consumerism proclaimed through powerful propaganda and religiously justified. It dominates not only the media in a constant stream of overwhelming commercial persuasion. It even usurps the language of the church in the so-called prosperity gospel, overturning the deepest meaning of the gospel

18. Wink, *Powers That Be*, p. 42.

Dare We Speak of Hope?

(saying that wealth is a blessing no matter how it is created and accrued). What the gospel presents as life-giving and life-enhancing is turned into the captivity of nihilism. What matters is not what we are meant to be — that is, created in the image of God — but what our material goods, our prosperity, and status determine us to be. It is not the image of God that determines our humanity; it is the brand we wear that determines our human-being-ness.

- It is the colonization of consciousness, values, and notions of human life by the imperial logic. This colonization of our mind, values, and notions of human life not only makes us susceptible to the logic of the empire, it robs us of what Walter Brueggemann calls our "prophetic imagination."[19] It robs us of our prophetic discernment and our prophetic critique, which spring from an *alternative consciousness*, one that serves to dismantle that very imperial consciousness that seeks to colonize our minds and our way of life. In resisting that imperial consciousness, we "nurture, nourish, and evoke a consciousness and perception alternative to the consciousness and perception of the dominant culture around us."[20]

- It is a spirit lacking compassionate justice and showing contemptuous disregard for the gifts of creation and the household of life. It seeks to convince us that seeking justice is unnecessary, immature, and futile. Justice — for the poor and defenseless, for the earth and for the excluded — is not a pursuable or reachable goal. Unlike the God of liberation, it cannot hear the cry of the oppressed; it refuses to see the destruction that its own rapaciousness and violence are

19. Walter Brueggemann, *The Prophetic Imagination* (Minneapolis: Fortress, 2001).
20. Brueggemann, *Prophetic Imagination*, p. 3.

causing; and it cannot respond with compassion and the doing of justice.

Looking back over the past decade or so, assessing our global situation, we would have to say that the churches who met at Accra in 2004 were correct. The times we live in indeed depict a "scandalous world" of harsh, utterly shocking, and growing inequalities across the world among and within nations; resource-driven wars; and poverty and disease, of which the most vulnerable victims are women and children.

Our global situation is one of enormous riches for those who run it and benefit from it. But for the poor and vulnerable, the neglected and the excluded, it constitutes an endless crisis, a constant battle for life. The hope for life "in all its fullness" and flourishing is almost impossible to see. Survival is the best they can do. The call is for the church to awaken in them the possibility to dream of a different world. That "dreaming a different world" is not a helpless wondering whether things will become better, nor an escape into a world where we resign ourselves to hopelessness because the dominant powers will not allow us to imagine a different world. It is, rather, "an assault on the consciousness of the empire, aimed at nothing less than the dismantling of the empire both in its social practices and in its mythic pretensions."[21]

A Scandalous World

Globally, inequalities have risen alarmingly.[22] The average North American consumes five times more than does a Mexi-

---

21. Brueggemann, *Prophetic Imagination*, p. 9.
22. For statistics and information on the next three paragraphs, see

can, ten times more than does a Chinese person, thirty times more than does an Indian. There are 1.3 billion people (22 percent of the world's population) living below the poverty line; 841 million are malnourished; 880 million are without access to medical care. One billion of the world's people lack adequate shelter; 1.3 billion have no access to safe drinking water; 2.6 billion go without sanitation. Among the children of the world, 113 million — two-thirds of them girls — go without schooling, and 150 million are malnourished. Thirty thousand die each day from preventable diseases. In eighteen countries, all of them in Africa, life expectancy is under fifty years (in Sierra Leone, it is a mere 37 years). Infant mortality rates are higher than one in ten in thirty-five countries, mostly in Africa, but including Bangladesh, Bolivia, Haiti, Laos, Nepal, Pakistan, and Yemen.

It gets worse. By the end of the second millennium CE, the top fifth of the world's population had 86 percent of the world's GDP, while the bottom fifth had just 1 percent. The inequalities become almost an absurdity. The assets of the world's three richest individual billionaires were more than the combined wealth of the 600 million inhabitants of the least-developed countries. Recently, world-renowned economist Joseph Stiglitz has made the point that the Walton family, the six heirs to the Walmart empire, "possess a combined wealth of some $90 billion, which is equivalent to the wealth of the entire bottom 30 percent of U.S. society."[23] And we now know that at least a billion persons across the globe go to bed hungry at night.

This is the "scandalous world" that the Accra Confession speaks of. In the language of that confession, we find the righ-

Jonathan Sacks, *The Dignity of Difference: How to Avoid the Clash of Civilizations* (New York and London: Continuum, 2006), p. 29.

23. Joseph Stiglitz, "The 1 Percent's Problem," *Vanity Fair*, June 2, 2012: readersupportednews.org/opinion2/279-82/11727-focus-the-1-percents-problem (accessed June 2, 2012).

teous anger and the prophetic courage that Saint Augustine made us aware of. For the language of Hope to be the language of life, both her children need to be recognized, embraced, and given voice to. But here is an important point: the Accra Confession speaks in this way because it sees the world not through the eyes of the powerful and privileged, but through the eyes of the poor and the suffering.

This is crucial, because in understanding this, we understand three key issues indispensable for the prophetic witness of the church in the world. First, by seeing the world through the eyes of those who suffer, we are seeing the world through the eyes of Jesus. When Jesus came into this world, he looked with the eyes of one born to a single mother, and, living under a cloud of scandal and disdain, as South African New Testament scholar Andries van Aarde describes him, "fatherless in Galilee."[24] He looked through the eyes of one born in a manger, in a stable, among the animals, the dirt and the dung, for whom there was no place in the respectable rooms of the inn. He looked through the eyes of a persecuted child, a refugee in hiding from the wrath of a vengeful, powerful but threatened monarch for whom spilling the blood of the innocent was simply a measure of self-protection. Jesus looked through the eyes of one who himself was poor, living among the poor and oppressed, the marginalized of Galilee and occupied Judea, those bowed down under the oppression of Roman domination and the exploitation of the temple elites.

Jesus looked through the eyes of one who was not understood or supported by his own family because they saw him as an embarrassment, constantly in conflict with the powers that determined life and death, someone who caused them fear,

24. See Andries van Aarde, *Fatherless in Galilee: Jesus as Child of God* (Harrisburg, PA: Trinity Press International, 2001).

anxiety, and uncertainty that they would rather live without. He was rejected by those for whom he brought the good news of God's choice for the poor and oppressed, those deemed unworthy by the powers. He looked through the eyes of one denied and betrayed by those he thought were his friends and disciples, hunted down, falsely accused, beaten, spat on, and crucified because of his obedience to God and his revolutionary challenge to the powerful. Those eyes saw the world differently than did the eyes of those looking through palace windows, from fortresses of safety and security, from the heights of arrogance and the gilded thrones of power and wealth.

The second thing we understand is the outrage of Jesus at the blatant injustice, the relentless oppression, the scandalous exploitation of the poor and vulnerable in Galilee and all of Judea. If we perceive this, we understand that Jesus was faithfully echoing the outrage of Yahweh that is expressed so vividly in the words of the prophets. Then we understand the flaming words of Matthew 23 and Jesus' anger at the elites who through the law extracted all they could from the poor, but missed "the weightier matters of the law: justice and mercy and faith" (Matt. 23:23).

In Mark 12:41-44, for instance, Jesus does not hold up the poor widow, who "out of her poverty has put in everything she has" as an example of "sacrificial giving," as we have so often told ourselves — and which the "prosperity gospelers" are exploiting with such scandalous skill. Rather, Jesus does it to "publicly denounce a system that made even those who had virtually nothing feel that they had to contribute their last bit or risk being excluded from God's blessings."[25] When Mark writes

25. Obery M. Hendricks, Jr., *The Politics of Jesus: Rediscovering the True Revolutionary Nature of Jesus' Teachings and How They Have Been Corrupted* (New York: Doubleday, 2006), p. 121.

that Jesus stations himself "opposite" the temple treasury, he is not simply talking space and position. He is talking *opposition:* opposition to exploitation, to abuse of the faith of the poor, to the false piousness that proffers avarice as devotion to God. No, it is not sentimental approval of baptized exploitation we are seeing here — it is divine outrage.

The temple tax system that made riches for the temple elite made victims of the poor. Jesus knew that what the people needed was to be freed from the awe of the temple, the temple system, and the power of the ruling elite "so that they might be free from their paralyzing fear of offending God by rejecting the caretakers of God's supposed house," writes New Testament scholar Obery M. Hendricks Jr., and he is right.

> This, then, was the meaning of Jesus' protest at the Temple: it was a repudiation of the Temple and those who ran it, repudiation of their abuse of the people's trust, their haughty dismissal of the people's worth, their turning the Temple of God into a profiteering enterprise, their exploitation of the people in the name of God and for the benefit of themselves and the Romans. It was a prophetic pronouncement to the priestly aristocracy that they must change or be judged by God.[26]

The third thing we see when looking through the eyes of those who suffer is their longing for justice, for the fulfillment of God's promises of justice in their life. With them, and through their struggles, says black theologian Dwight Hopkins of the African slaves, as well as of the oppressed in contemporary society, we discover that the Spirit of liberation with the oppressed in the Hebrew and Christian Scriptures is the same

26. Hendricks, *The Politics of Jesus*, p. 122.

Spirit laboring with the downtrodden and brokenhearted in the contemporary context today, because "we discover divine revelation wherever Jesus struggles with the marginalized as they move to co-constitute themselves into a new liberated full humanity."[27] With them we see the possibility of the impossible, the reality of things not seen but hoped for.

So, dare we speak of hope? Only if we speak of Hope's daughters. Only if we see the world and its systems of domination, oppression, and exploitation through the eyes of those who suffer – the poor, the vulnerable, the excluded, those considered less worthy. Dare we speak of hope? Only if we see the world and God's people through the eyes of Jesus, and only if we understand that following Jesus in his forgiveness of injustice means following Jesus in his outrage at injustice – that is, following Jesus in his love.

Dare we speak of hope? Only if we dare to be outraged at injustice and humiliation, at the assault on the creation of God, the dignity of God's children, and in that assault the assault on the worthiness of God. We dare speak of hope only if we have the courage to stand where God stands, to share in God's choice for the poor and lowly. Only if we know that hope, like grace, is not cheap – that such solidarity and such choices will mean that there is a price to be paid.

Dare we speak of hope? Only if we remember, as the "statement of discontent" says, that we are participants "in Jesus' mission of fullness of life for all creation." It is not *our* project, our plan, our vision. It is *Jesus'* mission in which we are called, by grace, to participate. Jesus is the center of our faith, of our longings for justice, and of our struggles for justice. So our "discontent" with the groaning of God's creation and the suffering

27. Dwight N. Hopkins, *Down, Up, and Over: Slave Religion and Black Theology* (Minneapolis: Fortress, 2000), p. 217.

of God's children; our "defiance" of the powers of domination that seek to rule God's world; our resistance to coercion and temptation to serve some other god; our "obligation" to speak the language of life to the world – all of that is caught up in our following of Christ. We are discontented because of God's discontent with injustice. We defy the powers because they seek to replace God in our lives. We are obligated to speak life because we serve a God of life, because our obligations are caught up in our obligation to obedience, love, and prophetic faithfulness – and because Jesus Christ is the life of the world.

CHAPTER THREE

Dare We Speak of Hope?
Only If We Speak of Struggle

"The only thing that stands between us and despair is the thought that Heaven has not yet failed us."

Sol Plaatje, 1916

"The road to freedom is via the CROSS."

Albert John Mvumbi Luthuli, 1958

"Between Us and Despair"

The words that lead us through our reflections in this chapter are from two stalwarts of the South African liberation struggle, from periods when the African National Congress, the main liberation movement in my country and the oldest on the continent, could count on strong, principled, Christian leadership. Sol Plaatje was the first secretary general of the ANC after its establishment in 1912, and Albert Luthuli its last president, before it was banned by the South African apartheid government in 1960. Both men were committed Christians whose faith in Jesus Christ was the foundation of their public witness and the inspiration for their participation in the struggle for freedom and justice. Let us first attend to the words of Sol Plaatje, spoken in 1916: "The only thing that stands between us and despair is the thought that Heaven has not yet failed us."

The year 1910 saw the establishment of the Union of South Africa, the realization of a dream for white South Africa, but a deal that excluded the vast majority of our people from the political dispensation – dispossessed of the vote, of power, of a dignified existence. We argued, pleaded, and petitioned the British crown in an effort to make them understand what an unmitigated disaster this would be, and how much such an unjust, politically shortsighted, and morally wrong arrangement would come to cost our country. All to no avail.

For the next eighty-four years – up until 1994 – this fraudulent pact of white racist solidarity, white political domination, and white economic interests would seal the fate of the democratic ideal in South Africa. It would spell untold misery for black people. The first land act came in 1913, enacted by the all-white Parliament, the first legalization of dispossession and land theft on a grand scale that had begun in 1652 with the dispossession and decimation of the first nations of South Africa, the Khoi and the San, and would end up in the establishing of the Bantustans and the fallacy of "white South Africa."[1]

1. The "Natives Land Act" stipulated that Africans could not acquire land outside the existing reserves and that non-Africans could not obtain land within the reserves. But in the terms of the act, the land available to Africans comprised only 7 percent of the total area of the country. Recommendations were later made for additional land. It was implemented in 1936, providing for much less land than originally allocated by the commission appointed for this task. In the end, Africans ended up with claim

In 1914, World War I broke out, and it was certain that no attention would be given to the plight of black and indigenous South Africans. The years 1914 and 1915 saw the so-called Boer rebellions, the armed uprisings of the white Afrikaners against the English colonial government: the Afrikaners were seeking to reestablish the Boer Republics as they were before the South African War (1899-1902) and to restore what they considered "their land." There is great and bitter irony here. The white settlers had just legalized one of the grandest schemes of land theft in modern history, and now they were fighting for their "God-given" land, without a thought that the land they were fighting for did not, in fact, belong to them. The real victims of dispossession, from the Cape Colony to the Far North, were left completely irrelevant to this struggle, their rightful ownership of the land of their ancestors unremembered, unheard, unacknowledged, and unheeded.

Therefore, in 1916, Sol Plaatje was surveying the consequences of all this: the destruction wrought by two and half centuries of slavery and racist despoliation; the devastation of dispossession; the physical, social, and psychological impact on people alienated from their land and bereft of livelihood, prospects, and – above all – dignity; the slow strangulation of creeping impoverishment; the deadly grip of political oppression, economic exploitation, and the dehumanization caused by legalized violence and state terror; the systematic diminishment of a people bereft of their sense of belonging. In the midst of these realities he spoke, and we knew that he was right: "The only thing that stands between us and despair is the thought that Heaven has not yet failed us." In the midst of all the chaos and pain of injustice, he knew and proclaimed – speaking hope and life to his people – that the God of whom Paul writes in

---

to ownership of 13 percent of the land. Millions of Africans were forced off their ancestral lands to make room for white settlers.

his letter to the Romans, the God of steadfastness and encouragement, of peace and hope, is there, standing between us and total despair (Rom. 15:5, 13, 33; 16:20).

Hope and Struggle

Even then — and throughout the protracted struggle for freedom and justice in South Africa — black people knew that without that life-giving hope we would not be able to hold out, to endure, to fight for a dream we could see but could not grasp, for a life we could not imagine but could only hope for, as we girded ourselves for continued struggle. And here again is the crucial lesson we have learned from Augustine: Hope is not an intellectual concept, something we comprehend after careful study, observed through the permutations of scientific analysis, created in esoteric academic debate. Hope is not a religious construct, disconnected from the lives and struggles of God's little people. No, Hope makes herself known *in encounter* with suffering and struggle. She emerges from within the struggle against the presence of evil and from within our engagement with the powers of domination and devastation. Hope teaches us that it is not our struggle, but that we join God in God's struggle for all of God's creation, not because we believe in a perfect world, but as Rubem Alves of Brazil has told us, because we believe that *this* imperfect order should not continue to exist.[2]

Hope does another thing. As she teaches us that it is not our struggle to claim, manipulate, and conduct as we will, she also teaches us that in this struggle we must not be beguiled, claimed, and deceived by the ideologies of this world, but that

2. See Rubem Alves, "Christian Realism: Ideology of the Establishment," *Christianity and Crisis*, September 17, 1973.

Dare We Speak of Hope?

we shall rather allow ourselves to be seduced by the dream of God for this world: the dream of justice, peace, humanity, solidarity, and wholeness. We must allow ourselves to succumb to the appeal from God. It is, as I have written elsewhere, an appeal that comes to us from the wounded other, the groaning earth and the crucified God, from the dream of God and the hopes of humanity, from the pain of the poor and the afflictions of the suffering Servant. This is what allows us to wax to our full humanity even as we struggle.

When we allow this to happen, it releases us from the compulsory revolutionary fervor that binds us more to the dictates of revolution than to the daily care for the lives and dignity of those who drive the revolution with their hopes, dreams, and sacrifices. "It frees us from the stifling rules of the revolution and from the bureaucratization of the mind, and opens us up to the liberating possibilities of fantasy and sensitivity in our obedience to God. It liberates us from the stranglehold of historical predetermination and sensitizes us to the eschatological possibilities as protest against empirical reality. It helps us to make the transition from self-righteous justification because we happen to benefit to that holy rage at the injustices which make us benefit. In short, it blesses us with the freedom of humanizing love."[3]

This is what happens if we allow ourselves to recognize that we are participating in Jesus' mission to create life and fulfillment.

Hope cannot be commissioned, called forth at will by the powerful for the legitimation of earthly power. Instead, Hope challenges earthly powers and principalities, and she places earthly powers under the critique of heaven and earth, by which

3. See Allan Boesak, *The Tenderness of Conscience: African Renaissance and the Spirituality of Politics* (Stellenbosch: Sun Media, 2005), pp. 222-23.

I mean the critique of the outraged God, the suffering people, and the ravaged earth. Her birthplace is not in the palaces of the privileged, nor the high-steepled, stained-glass-windowed sanctuaries of power and customized religiosity. Rather, her birthplace is under the bush in the wilderness, where Ishmael lies dying; under the broom tree, where Elijah wishes for death; in the flames of yet another bush, from which Yahweh speaks hope and life and liberation to Moses and his people with words of inextinguishable fire. Hope's birthplace is on that cross on the hill, where the cry "Eli, Eli, lema sabachthani?" is her form and shape. That is where Hope is born. When Hope speaks, she speaks not with the arrogance of certitude but with the eloquence of faith. She speaks with the voice of those whose voice is lost in the thunder of propaganda, those who have no voice because they are simply too tired, too lost, too weak, or too powerless to speak. Too unimpressive to be worth listening to, not hopeful of being heard, they are too discouraged to speak. She speaks for those whom the powerful have deprived of the right to speak.

Throughout centuries of struggle, oppressed people — and all those engaged in struggles for the sake of justice on their behalf — have intuitively understood this and have taken sustenance from it. For what is it, ultimately, that makes us endure? What gives us hope? What makes us stand up when we fall? What makes us go on when we are dragged down? What makes us believe that justice and peace shall become a reality, that no matter how hard the battle, how long the road, how deep the pain, or how dark the night, we shall overcome? And what makes those words not an empty, sentimental phrase from a song, but a commitment in body and soul not to give up until systems of oppression are broken down and justice is made a reality for all God's children?

It is the belief, the absolute conviction, that there is a God of justice, that that God has taken sides, and that that God calls us to join the struggle for justice and liberation. That God, the God of peace, encouragement, endurance, and hope, will, as Paul so boldly proclaims, give us the strength to fight on until Satan is "crushed under our feet" (Rom. 16:20).

We have known all along that what keeps us strong, what keeps us fighting, is the thought that the God of hope has not yet failed us. For when Sol Plaatje speaks of "Heaven," he speaks not of a distant mystical place. He speaks of the God of liberation, who said to Moses: "I have observed the misery of my people who are in Egypt; I have heard their cry on account of their taskmasters. Indeed, I know their sufferings, and I have come down to deliver them" (Exod. 3:7, 8).

This is the God who said to Pharaoh, "Let my people go!"
This is the God of Hannah: "For not by might does one prevail" (1 Sam. 2:9).
This is the God of Isaiah: "For the tyrant shall be no more!" (Isa. 29:20).
This is the God of Amos: "Let justice roll down like waters, and righteousness like a mighty stream" (Amos 5:24).
This is the God of Jesus: "The Spirit of the Lord is upon me, because he has anointed me to bring good news to the poor. He has sent me to proclaim release to the captives and recovery of sight to the blind, to let the oppressed go free, to proclaim the year of the Lord's favor" (Luke 4:18-19).

It is this God of whom Albert John Mvumbi Luthuli spoke when he led our people through the sustained nonviolent resistance campaign in the 1950s called the "Defiance campaign." The people in that campaign were inspired by their faith, nurtured by their hope, and strengthened by their dreams of justice. Luthuli himself was clear that he was in the struggle for justice precisely because he was a Christian, that it was his Christian faith that brought him there, and he faced the might of the apartheid regime with the conviction of the apostles in his heart: "We should obey God rather than human beings" (Acts 5:29). And as Hope emerges in struggle, she finds her place in radical obedience.

"It is my hope," Albert Luthuli said,

> that what began, in the way of Christian involvement and thinking out, at the time of the Defiance campaign, will not simply drain away, leaving Christians in despondency and impotence, adapting themselves fearfully to each new outrage, threat, and assault upon the people in our care. *There is a witness to be borne, and God will not fail those who bear it fearlessly.*[4]

That witness was borne not just by Christians, South Africans had discovered, but by people of other faiths as well, and by those with no faith in God at all, but bound together by the hope of a different future, not yet seen but dreamed of. Even as the white minority regime threw up the barricades, entrenched itself with even more draconian measures and ever-increasing violence, the people of South Africa gave shape to their hopes and dreams for justice and peace. In 1955, the masses of South Africans, white and black, came together in what would become the historic gathering at Kliptown, south of Johannesburg, now part of the region called Soweto. There they formulated and adopted what would become known as the "Freedom Charter," the document that charted a course for a new politics

4. Albert Luthuli, *Let My People Go! The Autobiography of Albert Luthuli* (Cape Town: Tafelberg, and Houghton: Mafube Publishers, 2006), pp. 23, 132 (italics added).

and laid the foundation for one of the most progressive documents of our time, the South African constitution.

"South Africa belongs to all who live in it, white and black," the document began, "and no government [can] justly claim authority unless it is based on the will of all the people. . . . We pledge ourselves to strive together sparing neither strength nor courage until the democratic changes here set out have been won."[5]

This is the language of pure hopefulness. There was nothing in the political reality of the times that gave those gathered at Kliptown reason to speak like this. They spoke the exact opposite of what apartheid was, and of what the apostles of apartheid were seeing and doing. But they hoped what could not be seen, they spoke into being what they dreamed of, and they made it a reality through their commitment, courage, and strength. They were bearing witness to the hope that was within them, uttering the shape of the future in words of faith in the midst of struggle.

"The Road to Freedom Is via the Cross"

Then an event occurred that would change the history of South Africa — and the struggle — dramatically. On March 21, 1960, the Pan Africanist Congress staged peaceful demonstrations in Johannesburg and Cape Town against the hated "pass laws," which represented a particularly pernicious piece of legislation controlling and severely restricting the movement of blacks, tearing families apart, and guaranteeing the humiliation of blacks at every turn. As the march approached the Sharpeville

5. The text of the Freedom Charter can be found at: http://www.anc.org
.za/show.php?id=72.

police station, near Johannesburg, police opened fire with live ammunition, killing 69 people and wounding over 186 others, most of them shot in the back. In the town of Evaton the protest was broken up by low-flying fighter jets, and in Langa, near Cape Town, 3 people were killed and 27 injured in a baton charge by police.

Government reaction was even harsher than before, and the cost of the resistance was high. A series of even more draconian laws were enacted, and liberation movements were banned, as were their leaders and many activists. Thousands were imprisoned. The "Treason" and "Rivonia" trials followed, in which, among others, Nelson Mandela was convicted and imprisoned for life. Others were forced into exile; all political activity was driven underground. In December 1960, the ANC made its historic decision to turn from nonviolent resistance to military action. This was not the desire of Albert Luthuli, who never condoned the use of violence. But as he mourned the tragic consequences of white racist intransigence, he understood the historical circumstances of a rabidly racist and power-hungry regime, and the longing of his people to be free.[6]

Luthuli himself remained banned and was under more and more pressure by the regime, finding it increasingly harder to

6. Despite recent, somewhat desperate attempts by ANC intellectuals and the leadership (including Nelson Mandela) to show that Luthuli was in full support of the decision to turn to violence, Scott Couper has argued convincingly that this was not the case. That Luthuli freely admitted that the violence and intransigence of the apartheid regime left him often unable to counter the arguments for violence does not make him an *advocate* for violence. His oft-quoted words are a cry of despair rather than a call for violence: "How long before, out of the depths [the oppressed people] cry, 'If the man of peace does not prevail, give us the men of blood?'" See Scott Couper, *Albert Luthuli: Bound By Faith* (Scottsville: University of KwaZulu-Natal Press, 2010), pp. 152-84.

Dare We Speak of Hope?

provide the leadership that the people needed now more than ever. Stripped of his position as chief, but not stripped of his faith, the banned leader of a banned organization, but not abandoned by God, he continued to speak the language of life to his people and the world. Standing under the shadow of the cross, his people under siege but not defeated, his dreams of freedom and his hope for reconciliation scorned but still embraced and held up to all of South Africa as our only future, Luthuli spoke new hope to his people: "The task is not yet finished. South Africa is not yet home for all her sons and daughters. Such a home we wish to ensure. . . ." Then he went on to speak the words that have emblazoned the banner of the struggle for nonracialism in South Africa ever since:

> From the beginning our history has been one of ascending unities, the breaking of tribal, racial and creedal barriers. The past cannot hope to have a life sustained by itself, wrenched from the whole. There remains before us the task of building a new land, a home for men [and women] who are black, white, brown, from the ruins of the old narrow groups, a synthesis of the rich cultural strains we have inherited. . . . Somewhere ahead there beckons a civilisation, a culture, which will take its place in the parade of God's history beside other great human syntheses. . . . It will not necessarily be all black; but it will be African.[7]

Such was the foresight of hope, the vision of the prophet.

When Luthuli testified at the trial of Nelson Mandela, he spoke of his dream for peace and freedom and called for negotiations. When the court, with the sarcasm of supreme political power, insisted that there was very little hope of that ever hap-

7. Albert Luthuli, *Let My People Go!* pp. 229-30.

pening, Luthuli responded, "There were no signs, my lords, in that direction . . . but hope is always there. . . ."[8] Even in those wretched circumstances, when the powers that be insisted on what *they* saw as South Africa's future, Luthuli refused to let go of his hope for peace, dignity, and life for all of South Africa's people. Even while he could foresee that "the present and the immediate future are pregnant with anguish and pain for all . . . in South Africa," all the while he stood by what he said and understood in 1958, that it would be costly: "The road to freedom is via the CROSS."[9]

In his written statement, Luthuli spells the word "cross" with capital letters. The cross he is speaking of, he wants us to understand, is not the cross we wear for ornamentation; it is not the cross of the commonplace wisdom that every human being carries because we are human, sharing the common ailments and everyday burdens of humanity; it is certainly not the cross that, together with the sword, emblazoned the standards of the empire and blessed Western Christendom's sinful alliances of throne and altar as Jesus became the divine justifier of war, oppression, conquest, and domination. Rather, he is speaking of the cross to which Jesus was condemned as a result of his resistance, of his revolutionary actions, and of his stand against the powers of domination and destruction in his day. It is the cross Jesus invites his followers to take up and carry, in obedience and with the certainty of suffering, in courage and the hope that through the vulnerability and the power of this cross, victory shall be assured and the world would become the domain of God's justice.

8. "Testimony in the Treason Trial, March 1960 (extracts)": http://www .anc.org.za/ancdocs/history/lutuli/lutulii8.html#six8 (accessed April 6, 2012). Also cited by Kader Asmal, "Introduction," Albert Luthuli, *Let My People Go!*, p. xxi.

9. Luthuli, *Let My People Go!*, pp. 230, 232-36.

This is not the Jesus whose name was carved on the sides of the slave ship that carried our African ancestors across the ocean into perpetual slavery. This is not the Jesus in whose name we were conquered, enslaved, disinherited, and dismembered — unnamed, renamed, and baptized, not as members of his church but as chattel in captivity. For even as we were baptized, we were branded.[10]

Luthuli's Jesus was the Jesus upon whom the Spirit of the Lord rests, the one who came to bring good news to the poor, to proclaim liberty to the captives, and to let the oppressed go free. He is the one who announced the favorable Year of the LORD, who brought the soft yoke and the light burden of mercy, justice, and love. Luthuli's Jesus was the one whose lordship declared null and void the false claims of lordship made by the emperor, exposed the pretenses of those in authority, and turned on its head the meaning of power. This Jesus shunned the violence of power and domination by accepting the violence of the cross inflicted on himself on Good Friday and rising from the grave on Sunday, thereby forever delegitimizing — no, nullifying — the power of violence. He is the one who stepped outside the safety and comfort of the camp, stood by the side of those who were despised, rejected, exploited, and deemed unworthy, and he shared their humiliation and their pain and brought them hope for life. Jesus, Luthuli knew, as did Isaiah, is "the Servant whom Yahweh has chosen," the one Yahweh loves and in whom Yahweh delights:

10. "When a planter bequeathed his estate in Barbados [to the Society for the Propagation of the Christian Gospel of the Church of England], the new owners had the word 'Society' branded on the chest of each of its newly acquired slaves to affirm the possession" (Gerard L'Ange, *The White Africans: From Colonisation to Liberation* (Johannesburg and Cape Town: Jonathan Ball Publishers, 2005), p. 20.

I will put my Spirit on him,
   and he will proclaim justice to the nations.
He will not quarrel or cry out;
   no one will hear his voice in the streets.
A bruised reed he will not break,
   and a smoldering wick he will not snuff out,
till he has brought justice through to victory.
   In his name the nations will put their hope.
                              (Matt. 12:18-21 [NIV]; cf. Isa. 42:1-4)

The Place Where Christ Stands

But Hope is found where Jesus is to be found, this Jesus who was
despised and rejected, whose countenance, like the faces of the
wretched of the earth, no one desires to gaze upon. Our decisions about the fundamental and ultimate issues of life, writes
Dietrich Bonhoeffer, that great theologian of the resistance
against Nazism (whose views on this matter I promised to return to), must always lead us to the place "where Christ stands."
Speaking in 1928 to his expatriate German congregation in Barcelona, Spain, Bonhoeffer said:

> The question before us is whether in our own day Christ still
> stands in the place where decisions are made concerning the
> most profound matters we are facing, namely concerning
> our own lives and the life of our people [the *Volk*] . . . whether
> the Spirit of Christ can still speak to us of the ultimate, final,
> decisive matters.[11]

11. Dietrich Bonhoeffer, *Barcelona, Berlin, New York: 1928-1931*, Clifford J. Green, ed., Dietrich Bonhoeffer Works, vol. 10 (Minneapolis: Fortress, 2008), p. 342.

That place, says Bonhoeffer, is with "the children and the morally and socially 'least of these,' those viewed as less worthy." Following this logic — namely, the logic of Christ — Bonhoeffer found that place beyond his own life and the life of his people (the *Volk*). He found it with "the children," because they were the most vulnerable and most neglected, most easily forgotten victims of war; with those whom the Nazis considered "less worthy" (Jews, gypsies, gays, communists, the disabled); and later with those who joined the resistance against Hitler and the Nazis. But there, in those dangerous and threatened places, was where Christ was to be found. No wonder Bonhoeffer talked about Jesus Christ as at the very center of this decision, Christ himself representing "an all or nothing decision."[12]

This is where Christ is still to be found today. Outside the comfort and protection of the camps of privilege, comfort, and entitlement; exposed and vulnerable along the Jericho road; outside the city wall, where the lepers and the demon-possessed are forced to dwell; in the lanes and alleys, where the prostitutes wait to be noticed, used, and discarded; among the exploited multitudes, "like sheep without a shepherd," who hunger and thirst for justice.

This is where Jesus is to be found and where Hope waits to be recognized today: in the ghettos and squatter camps where poverty, hunger, and neglect reign supreme; in the silent and suffocating enclosures of domestic and sexual violence, where fear has dislodged love and mutual respect; in the public spaces where justice is perverted so that the poor and powerless suffer; out on the hill where the crosses are planted, on which hang the innocent, the defenseless, and the resisters who defend the

12. See Ferdinand Schlingensiepen, *Dietrich Bonhoeffer, 1906-1945: Martyr, Thinker, Man of Resistance* (London and New York: T&T Clark, 2010), p. 49.

innocent. Where hopelessness claims the throne and despair proclaims supremacy, there Hope is waiting to be embraced, to be invited into the struggle for justice.

It is in the lived encounter with suffering and pain, in the heat of struggle with powers of evil that Hope emerges, where she takes shape and form, reaches out to hold us fast. Holding onto her hand, we discern the power of her presence in the testimony of the ancients, the words of the prophets, and the life and the gospel of Jesus of Nazareth, the Word of life that cannot be bound, that empowers and enables for justice and freedom and fullness of life.

As believers today, we are deeply connected to that company of faith, "that cloud of witnesses" who held fast onto Hope in the most trying of circumstances. We are bound by the same Spirit. Carried and sustained by their faithfulness and clinging to Hope's hand, we walked the wilderness and drank the water from the angel's hand with Hagar; we climbed the mountaintop with Moses and saw the Promised Land; we slept under the broom tree with a desperately fearful Elijah and experienced the awesome presence of God, not in the wind or the fire, but in the sound of a gentle whisper. We shed tears in the temple with Hannah and wept with Elisha, dreading the coming destruction. With the psalmist, our voice cried out to heaven: "How long, LORD?" And we believed, as John Calvin taught us, that it is as if the Lord hears the cry of God's own heart when *we* cry out, "How long?" Reminding us in radical terms of where God stands in the struggles and longing for justice in our world – and it is as if he is speaking of our imperial reality today – Calvin writes:

> When anyone disturbs the whole world by his ambition and avarice, or everywhere commits plunders, or oppresses miserable nations – when he distresses the innocent, all cry out, How long? And this cry, proceeding as it does from the feeling of nature and the dictate of justice, is at length heard

Dare We Speak of Hope?

by the Lord. . . . [The oppressed] know that <u>this confusion</u> good
<u>of order</u> and justice is not to be endured. And this feeling,
is it not implanted in us by the Lord? It is then the same as
though God hears [Godself], when [God] hears the cries and
groaning of *those who cannot bear injustice.*[13]

We wept with Rachel and refused to be comforted, because
our children, too, were no more. With Isaiah and Jeremiah we
heard – and believed – the promise of justice, salvation, and
restoration, and with Amos we vowed not to rest until justice
rolls down like waters and righteousness like a mighty stream.
With Mary we sang the Magnificat, and with Jesus we suffered
on a cross made by human hands. With the women we stood
by the cross and with them we went to the grave and saw the
empty tomb; we received the good news from the angel and we
hastened to tell the world that Christ had risen. In prison we
learned to sing with Paul and Silas, and with the ancient church
we denounced imperial idolatry when we discovered that there
is no lord but Jesus; and with Paul we were convinced that "neither death, nor life, nor angels nor rulers, nor things present,
nor things to come, nor powers, nor height, nor depth, nor
anything in all creation will be able to separate us from the love
of God in Jesus Christ our Lord" (Rom. 8:38-39).

Singing with Hope

<u>One of Hope's greatest gifts</u>, we had learned, is that she puts
<u>song into our mouths</u>. She teaches us to sing in those moments

13. John Calvin, *Commentaries on the Twelve Minor Prophets*, vol. 4:
Habakkuk, Zephaniah, Haggai (Grand Rapids: Eerdmans, 1950), pp. 93-94
(italics added).

when we think that music is betrayal, melody is heresy, and singing is unthinkable. Hope teaches us that a song can sing the present as it is and the future as it should be, and that if we could only learn to sing it, we could make it happen. This was, and remains, one of the greatest, most moving and inspirational — and for the apartheid regime, most unnerving — characteristics of the struggle against apartheid. We called them "freedom songs." We sang of freedom while freedom was nowhere in sight and apartheid was in full bloom. Against indescribable odds we stood and fought for justice, freedom, and dignity in the darkest days of apartheid, during successive states of emergency, and we faced dogs and guns and tear gas. We went to prison and were tortured; many of our comrades disappeared, and many were also killed on the streets as they marched and confronted apartheid's military might; many saw death in torture chambers. Our schools became battlegrounds, and our township streets became killing fields. We struggled against the forces of forgetfulness, and we resisted the powers of unremembering.[14] We went from funeral to funeral, in the words of nineteenth-century poet and hymn-writer John Ntsikana,

> fearful of the thoughts till now never spoken,
> making shreds of our innermost being . . .
> [journeying] with us to the grave,
> encircled by a smiling Gospel.[15]

14. For the use of this term, see Allan Aubrey Boesak, *The Tenderness of Conscience*, pp. 103ff.

15. From the poem "The Shade of a Fabulous Ghost," written in 1884 by John Ntsikana, blind catechist and the first African on the subcontinent to compose Christian hymns; quoted in Es'kia Mphahlele, *ES'KIA, Education, African Humanities and Culture, Social Consciousness, Literary Appreciation* (Johannesburg: Kwela Books, 2002), p. 298; see also Boesak, *The Tenderness of Conscience*, pp. 136-37.

Dare We Speak of Hope?

And then Hope taught us to sing. We saw pain and death, and we sang, *Senzenina* ("What have we done?"). We could not understand why the color of our skin was such a sin against God. We saw the dreams and hopes of our children dissolving into blood and tears, and we sang, *Tuma mina, tuma mina, tuma mina, Nkosi Yam* ("Send me, Lord"). Even if I am afraid, send me, Lord. Even if I never see my home again, send me, Lord. Even if I have to walk through the valley of the shadow of death, send me, Lord. Let me not wait upon others. Send *me*, Lord. And we saw Hope making her way through and rising above the hate and the violence and the cruelty and the stench of fear and death. We took her hand and we sang, our joy transcending and transforming our fear: *Ukanamandla, ukanamandla, ukanamandla, uSatani!* ("It is broken, it is broken, the power of Satan – it is broken! Hallelujah!") The struggle was not yet won; it was far from over. And not all of us would see the victory; many would not come out of the wilderness. But we held onto Hope, and in turn Hope embraced us, and we knew it was certain, that nothing could stop it: *Ukanamandla, uSatani!*

Grieving with God

But Dietrich Bonhoeffer teaches us yet another truth as we join God's struggle for justice and learn to stand where God stands. To stand where God stands, to make decisions that would take us to where Christ is to be found, namely, with the wronged, the destitute, the poor, the marginalized, those "less worthy," means infinitely more. It means, Bonhoeffer tells us, "to stand with God in the hour of God's grieving."[16] With that,

16. Dietrich Bonhoeffer, *Letters and Papers from Prison*, John W. De-

Bonhoeffer invites us into the depths of even greater myster-
ies. We stand not only by those who are grieved and wronged
through injustices and suffering, but we stand by *God*, since
God is grieving because of their grief. But to be able to do that,
we must be "caught up in the way of Christ." "Caught up" here
means "wholly committed to," driven by that radical, sacrificial
obedience Bonhoeffer so often talks about. It is not our religion,
Bonhoeffer insists, that makes of us believers and followers of
Christ. Rather, it is our participation in the suffering of God.
Grieving with God is not a passive state of mourning, of helpless resignation. It is walking the way of Christ, "caught up" in
the way of Christ, looking at the world and at people through
the eyes of the suffering Servant. It calls us not just to tears but
to activist discipleship. "Sharing" in the grief of God is rising up
against whatever causes God to grieve, namely, the needless
suffering of God's children and God's earth.

We are called to share in the grief of God as God suffers at
the hands of a hostile world — "hostile" because the world God
loves has turned against God and resists God's plans for wholeness and justice and peace. That world is profiting from the suffering of God's children and the ravaging of God's creation. Understanding that, Bonhoeffer maintains, is what distinguishes
us from pagans: that is, we know that God is grieving at the
pain of God's world. It does not distinguish us from people of
other faiths. No, this sensitivity, this awareness of God's grieving, distinguishes us from pagans, and these are those who
in their worship of possessions and positions despise the love
of God and shun the worship of God, those who place profits
above people, the greed and gratification of the moment above
the sacredness of creation and the needs of generations to come.

Gruchy, ed., Dietrich Bonhoeffer Works, vol. 8 (Minneapolis: Fortress,
2010), pp. 515-16.

They are truly those whom Paul had in mind: "They were filled with every kind of wickedness, evil, covetousness, malice. Full of envy, murder, strife, deceit, craftiness, they are gossips, slanderers, God-haters, insolent, haughty, boastful, inventors of evil, rebellious toward parents, foolish, faithless, heartless, ruthless" (Rom. 1:29-31). These are the pagans Bonhoeffer chastises here: those who call themselves Christians but for whom their religiosity, their symbols, and their rituals have become the hallmark of their life, those who think that it is more important to be religious than to be followers of Christ. The grief they cause the world is the grief with which God mourns. We are not called to be religious. We are called to be disciples of Christ. And we are disciples of Christ when we stand by God in the hour of God's grieving. The grieving of God is not in the pain of God for God, but in the pain of God in the suffering of humanity and the destruction of God's earth. The pain inflicted by humanity's inhumanity toward humanity, the pain that comes when the earth is ravaged — that is, the pain inflicted on God. When Bonhoeffer speaks of the pain of God, he does not search the heavens to look for God; he looks around him at the pain of people created in the image of God, meant for joy and love and fulfillment of life. When we fail to stand with them, we fail to stand with God. This is the other side of our glorying in God.

We do not ask whether their pain is the pain of those who differ from us, or of persons of other faiths. The pagan within us is who asks that. We stand by them because their pain is the pain of a grieving God. That is discipleship, because it is being caught up in the way of Jesus Christ. And that is where we will find Hope.

So this is where Hope and our struggle with her bring us: standing where Christ stands, sharing the grief of God, and standing on the justice of God, we stand with Hope.

We stand with the poor, the exploited, and the vulnerable, the destitute, the wronged, and the needy — and we hold up their needs as holy before God.

We stand with the Palestinians as they grieve and protest the loss of land, rights, and future, struggling for some semblance of hope against the uncaring powerful of the world, suffering in the shadow of the Wall — and we hold up their needs as holy before God.

We stand with the people of the Pacific Islands, victims, first of colonization and despoliation, of nuclear testing and toxic waste, and now of ecological disaster and rising sea levels — and we hold up their needs as holy before God.

We stand with the women, abused and dishonored, who cannot find succor nor safety in a church held captive by patriarchal power — and we hold up their needs as holy before God.

We stand with the children who are cannon fodder for war and child-soldiers who are shields for the cravers of power and who feed off war and profit from war — and we hold up their needs as holy before God.

We stand with the women and children, boys and girls who are lost, preyed on, caught, and trafficked, sold into new and frightening forms of slavery — and we hold up their needs as holy before God.

We stand with the Dalits and Tribals of India, declared untouchable by human law and religious custom, but touched, embraced, and redeemed by God in Jesus Christ — and we hold up their needs as holy before God.

We stand with the hungry and neglected and forsaken of the world, whose hunger and thirst for food and water are as real and as sacred as their hunger and thirst for justice and compassion — and we hold up their needs as holy before God.

We stand with the lesbians and gays and all persons who are not heterosexual, who are scorned, derided, and denied, in whom God's image is despised, those who are hunted and battered, and raped and murdered just because God made them different — and we hold up their needs as holy before God.

We stand with those who suffer from HIV and AIDS, for whom battling the illness is as painful as bearing the stigma — and we hold up their needs as holy before God.

We stand with the powerless everywhere, whose powerlessness leaves them with no options, no choices, and no recourse — and we hold up their needs as holy before God.

We stand with Mother Earth, raped and ravaged, whose mountains and hills are bleeding wounds, whose rivers weep filth and pollution, whose oceans are impregnated with death — and we hold up her needs as holy before God.

We stand with all those who have the righteous anger and the courage to stand in solidarity of struggle in the hope of the fulfillment of life — and we hold up their needs as holy before God.

If we stand with all of the above, we will find hope, we will walk with Jesus, caught up in the way of discipleship, and we will speak the language of hope and life.

CHAPTER FOUR

Dare We Speak of Hope?

Only If We Speak of Seeking Peace

"I believe that the potential destructiveness of modern weapons today rules out the possibility of war ever again achieving a negative good. If we assume that [humankind] has a right to survive, then we must find an alternative to war and destruction. . . . The choice is either non-violence or non-existence."

Martin Luther King Jr.

"When hope dies, the pregnant mother of time dies with the unborn child of a redeemed future."

J. Alfred Smith Sr.

"Like a seedling, with sun, good soil, and abundant rain, the roots of our future will bury themselves in the ground and a canopy of hope will reach into the sky."

Wangari Maathai

"The Glory That Is Not Steeped in Blood"

It seems as though the presence of war is the one enduring constant in the developing history of humankind. Even as enlightened science brought new possibilities for meaningful life such as we have never seen, our capacity for creating death has become even more resourceful. Every medical wonder enhancing the opportunities for human development seems to be eclipsed by the sophistication of our means of war, leaving us all to wonder at the true meaning of "progress." Scientific ingenuity increasingly in the service of the means of death has left us all bewildered and disoriented.

World War I, "the war to end all wars," seems to have taught humankind nothing about our capacity for evil, as World War II brought us face to face with even greater depths of evil. The era of nuclear deterrence between East and West, known as the cold war, was without a doubt an unnerving period for the countries of the North, but for the countries of the global South it was never "cold." Wars of liberation and independence, forced on the natives of colonized lands by recalcitrant and greedy colonial masters – from Africa to Southeast Asia – caused death and destruction without measure. While the war against Vietnam, Laos, and Cambodia became the epitome of Western postcolonial aggression, Africa and the Middle East became the paradigm for proxy wars by both East and West, as nationalist groups were pitted against each other in efforts to protect and promote either Eastern or Western interests.

As I write, Somalia and the Democratic Republic of Congo are embroiled in ongoing civil wars that seem to have no end. In other places, such as Uganda, Rwanda, and post-Gaddafi Libya, war never seems far off, and the simmering tensions make a peaceful life impossible. Africa's people search the skies in vain for that canopy of hope under whose shade they can find peace and sustainable, abundant life.

State terror over decades, particularly by countries such as Russia, the United States, and Israel, has called forth the terror of stateless groups who wage war for other reasons than defense of country. As much as have modern technology and the monumental changes in geopolitics since 1989, this has completely changed the nature of war.

But not everything is as new as one might be inclined to think. Because wars against colonized peoples were always considered "wars against uncivilized adversaries," the so-called laws of war, either in the form of international law or that of the just-war theory as applied by Christian thinkers for centuries, did not apply. The extermination of the "lower races" was seen as a biological, political, and economic necessity. In these wars, "brutality," "accountability" and "proportionate response" as so-called measures of restraint did not exist. From early on in modern times, colonial wars were the experimental fields of extinction.

The first bomb dropped from an airplane, writes historian Sven Lindqvist, was Italian, and it exploded on November 1, 1911, in an oasis outside Tripoli, North Africa. The first systematic aerial bombing was carried out by the British Royal Air Force against the Somalis in 1920.[1] The particular — and unforgettable — horror of the Holocaust was the fact that the Jewish people were to be exterminated *as a whole*. That was indeed unique, but only for Europe. "The Holocaust," Lindqvist writes, "was born at the meeting point of two traditions that marked modern Western civilization: the anti-Semitic tradition and

1. Quoted in Mahmood Mamdani, *Good Muslim, Bad Muslim: America, the Cold War and the Roots of Terror* 4th ed. (Johannesburg: Jacana Media, 2007), p. 7. Africa's first genocide was, of course, experienced by the Khoi and the San, the first nations of South Africa, through the colonization process led by the Dutch in the seventeenth century, followed by the English in 1804. Hereafter, page references to this work appear in parentheses in the text.

the tradition of genocide of colonised peoples" (p. 7). The first genocide of the twentieth century was the German annihilation of the Herero people in erstwhile South West Africa (today Namibia) in 1904 (p. 7). The German geneticist Eugen Fischer's first medical experiments focused on a "science" of race-mixing in concentration camps set up for the Herero people. His subjects were both Herero and the mixed-parentage offspring of Herero-Germans, who were, Fischer argued, physically and mentally inferior to their German parents. Adolf Hitler appointed Fischer rector of the University of Berlin, and one of Fischer's prominent students there was Joseph Mengele (p. 8).

This helps us gain some perspective on modern terrorism, but it also has consequences for our theological reflection on the issues of global terror in our globalized world today, as well as for our moral judgments on war in general, and on the "war on terror." Ugandan political scientist and anthropologist Mahmood Mamdani, of Makarere University, makes the observation in his very thoughtful study of the roots of terrorism, that anticolonial violence, as a response to the violence of the colonial system, is not an irrational, premodern manifestation, but it "belongs to the script of modernity and progress, that it is indeed a midwife of history" (p. 9). Such violence is also a warning, he writes, "that more than celebrate this turning of the tables, we need to think through the full implications of victims becoming killers." The truth of this statement causes us to pause when we reflect on events twenty-five years ago in Cambodia, more recently in Rwanda, and in the Israeli actions in the Gaza strip.

I write these first paragraphs not only to highlight the complexity of the issues under discussion, but also to mark the difference that one's perspective makes in the discussion.

Let me declare myself: I approach this discussion as a Christian liberation theologian from the global South, and more as a spiritual child of Erasmus of Rotterdam than of Martin Luther and John Calvin; more a child of Mohandas Gandhi, Albert Luthuli, and Martin Luther King Jr. than of Frantz Fanon and Ché Guevara. I am much more uplifted by the song of Hannah (1 Sam. 2) than by the song of Deborah (Judges 5); much less attracted by the militance of King David and more to the revolutionary nonconformism of Jesus of Nazareth; much less drawn by the throne-and-altar religiosity of Western Christianity than by the nonviolent devotion of the early Christian church.

The wisdom of Erasmus of Rotterdam, that great humanist of the sixteenth century, speaks of his hope that we would not "seek the glory that is steeped in blood" as he admonishes the "truly Christian prince" to first of all weigh the great difference between a human being, "who is a creature born for peace and good will, and beasts and monsters, who are born to predatory war . . . how earnestly peace is to be sought and how honorable and welcome it is . . . [to keep in mind that] even if victory is certain, victory does not always happen to favor the best causes. . . . Let the good prince establish matters of the sort that will be of lasting worth."[2]

The Dimensions of Megaterrorism

Since the beginning of the millennium, we have seen a new phenomenon arising within our new globalized realities. International law expert and United Nations adviser Richard Falk has established what he calls "the dimensions of megaterrorism." He defines megaterrorism as a "unique challenge, differ-

2. Erasmus, "On Beginning War," in "The Education of a Christian Prince," extracts in Arthur F. Holmes, ed., *War and Christian Ethics* (Grand Rapids: Baker, 1975), pp. 177-78.

ing from earlier expressions of global terrorism, by magnitude, scope, and ideology, representing a serious effort to transform the world as a whole, and not merely change the power structure of one or more sovereign states."[3]

Falk comes with strong credentials. He is, by his own admission, a "consistent and harsh critic" of U.S. foreign policy, especially pertaining to the "Washington consensus," its "capital-driven focus on economic growth, and its tendency to widen income gaps between North and South, as well as to ignore persisting poverty and longer-term environmental decay." He also has continued to oppose "the main directions of American foreign policy despite the changing global agenda." The result of this critical engagement was conditional approval of U.S. actions regarding Kosovo, for example. The text I will use to follow Falk's thinking in this matter is his book *The Great Terror War*, which seeks to "clarify" what Falk believes to have been "an appropriate response to September 11," and even though "it is not in any sense intended to give a stamp of approval to what President Bush has done up to now," the book accepts "the main rhetorical and tactical thrust of the initial policy of American response, although only partially . . ." (p. xxii). In Falk's view, "the exercise of such a U.S. right of self-defense seemed valid and necessary despite the existence of the legitimate grievances in the Arab world . . ." (p. 30), because September 11 "has changed everything, forever!" as he, with some understanding, quotes the American leadership (p. 38).

Falk mentions seven dimensions of megaterrorism: the symbolism of the magnitude of the attacks and the targets chosen; the severity of effects; the genocidal intent; the visionary

3. Richard Falk, *The Great Terror War* (New York: Olive Branch Press, 2003), p. 39. Hereafter, page references to this work appear in parentheses in the text.

goals of the terrorists; their tactical ingenuity; their unconditional motivation; and their resonant message. He speaks of the "sheer numbers [of victims] involved" (scaled back from over 6,000 initially to slightly fewer than 3,000) and the loss of life of several hundred New York City fire fighters and police officers, "who sacrificed their own lives . . ." (p. 39).

The symbolic effects were "shattering": the twin towers and the Pentagon. What was at stake was "civilization," or as some interpreted it, even "modernity" itself. Important also was the sense of insecurity and the realization that "the inner core of the American colossus was severely vulnerable" (p. 41).

The genocidal character of this terrorism "intensifies the dangers posed," takes on a "depraved character," and certainly qualifies as a "crime against humanity." The religious dimension is reflected in the vision so uniquely captured by the very word *jihad* and held before all the world in the words of Osama bin Laden: "[I]t is our duty to make *jihad* so that God's word is the only one exalted to the heights and so that we drive the Americans away from all Muslim countries" (p. 43).

As Palestinian intellectual Edward Said has observed, bin Laden's message was visionary: "It transcended the political and moved to the metaphysical. There was a kind of cosmic, demonic quality of mind at work here, which refused to have any interest in dialogue and political organization and persuasion" (p. 49).

The tactical ingenuity could be seen in the "extraordinary execution of the operation." It was "staggering" and exposed the inadequacy of the weaponry of the modern state. "Striking back at what? To what end?" Falk asks. In addition, the terrorists had something few others could match: "The devastation of September 11 was crucially dependent on the dedication of the participants and their capacity to remain focused on a suicidal mission over a period of several years . . ." (pp. 53-55).

Falk knows that the American response, reducing the whole matter to George Bush's question, "Why do they hate us?" is "diversionary rhetoric" to make the resonance of bin Laden's message "disappear from political consciousness" (p. 57). Even though Falk knows that such an "attempted deflection of Islamic resentment ['they hate our freedoms . . .'] is profoundly misleading," he cautions that it would be equally misleading "to suggest that there is not an Islamic dimension of encounter that could move either toward accommodation or degenerate in the direction of a 'clash of civilizations'" (pp. 56, 57). But already we should be more cautious. Bin Laden's appeal is to a certain interpretation of Islam and a one-sided emphasis on jihad, ignoring jihad as spiritual battle and stretching the tradition of jihad as self-preservation and self-defense.[4] As in Christian fundamentalist thinking, such interpretations of sacred texts are not at all new and have the same disastrous consequences.

Falk points out how our globalized reality has further changed the nature of war. Globalization has brought about a dramatic shift in national identity, national loyalties, and citizenship. In our new reality, the psychological foundations of group and national identity may not correspond with state boundaries, creating a variety of tensions (p. 134). In fact, "one impact of globalization and the rise of regional political communities has been to establish multiple identities and a non-exclusive sense of citizenship" (p. 135).

Falk is right, but it is true of not just "regional political communities," in my opinion. There is such a thing as "transnational political communities," bound together not by national

4. See Irfan A. Omar, "Islam," in Miguel A. De La Torre, ed., *The Hope of Liberation in World Religions* (Waco, TX: Baylor University Press, 2008), p. 104: "Jihad is not a struggle to promote one's own interest or for political gain; rather it must be taken up for promoting the cause of the oppressed and the weak."

symbols, national political realities or national patriotism, traditionally understood as "love of country." These come in all kinds of permutations and causes held dear by convictions — political or religious or both — and have strong appeal across national borders or affiliations. These are rooted in notions of solidarity based on shared experiences, a common vision, and beliefs and values that resonate more deeply than exclusive territorial preoccupations. This surely must be a considerable strength in the message of Al Qaeda and its resonance across so many nationalities.

In this regard, Mahmood Mamdani makes another important — and well-known — point that became crystallized out of the Afghan War. "The CIA," he points out, "was key to the forging of the link between Islam and terror in central Asia and to giving radical Islamists international reach and ambition. The terrorists it trained and sponsored shared a triple embrace: of terror tactics, of holy war as a political ideology, and of transnational recruitment of fighters, who acquired hyphenated identities." The Afghan jihad went further, linking together an "international jihadi vanguard of Algerian-Afghans, Egyptian-Afghans, Indonesian-Afghans, Filipino-Afghans, British-Afghans, and so on. The importance of the vanguard was that its members shared an experience that shaped their ideological and political perspective."[5] In other words, all those other nationalities that Mamdani mentions, took on the Afghan identity, in solidarity of suffering and the sharing of a common vision and a common cause. The shared experience Mamdani speaks of is not just local, and even though local issues remain important, the issues of transnational solidarity transcended them.

In fact, local situations reinforced the transnational, validating them. In the notorious Osama bin Laden recruitment

5. Mamdani, *Good Muslim, Bad Muslim*, p. 163.

video, televised after 9/11, he did not once refer to the internal "freedoms" of the USA. What stood central in his remarks, rather, was what he had to say about Islam and the Arab world, and those pictures of Mohammed al-Durra, the twelve-year-old Palestinian boy shot by Israeli soldiers, dying in his father's arms, and of the Iraqi babies dying of malnutrition in under-equipped hospitals, crippled by American-driven sanctions. The fact that these fighters were British or Egyptian or Indonesian mattered less than their identification with Afghanistan, what Afghanistan has come to symbolize, and their shared belief in a version of Islam that enabled them to respond the way they do.

A View from Below

Throughout this book I have argued for the "view from below": seeing the world through the eyes of those who are the victims of violence that society justifies. Rahul Mahajan represents such a view as he looks at our subject from below. "The world changed on September 11," writes Mahajan, another American and representative of the antiwar movement in the United States, on that point agreeing with Falk. But he offers a different perspective from Falk's.[6] For a start, unlike most commentators on the subject, he mentions that on that day the phrase "Today, we are all Americans" echoed around the world, and not just the Western world. The community of nations "was realized in shared grief," and leaders from Yasser Arafat to Cuban Foreign Minister Felipe Perez Roque to Mohammad Khatami of Iran ex-

6. Rahul Mahajan, *The New Crusade: America's War on Terrorism* (New York: Monthly Review Press, 2002). Hereafter, page references to this work appear in parentheses in the text.

pressed their rejection of acts of terrorism "wherever they may come from." Even Wakil Ahmed Mutawakil, the Taliban's foreign minister, denounced the terrorist attack (p. 7).

For Mahajan, 9/11 forever ended the idea that the United States could somehow float above the rest of the earth, "of it and not of it at the same time. . . . It is more crucial than ever that we understand what kind of world we are living in, and what the United States has done to make it so" (p. 8). He raises questions not only about the truth in the version of events given by the U.S. government and the U.S. media, but he uses a wider lens: "What is the larger historical context in which the war on terrorism can be understood and assessed?" (p. 8). Like Falk, he understands the war on terror as an element of U.S. imperial ideology, but sees in it a "new kind of cultural supremacism." Mahajan puts forward the idea of "a new white man's burden" (p. 8),[7] and links it with America's "easy demonization of Third World peoples, especially of Arabs," and its urge to "excommunicate from humanity whoever happens to be the foe at the moment . . ." (p. 13).

Mahajan assumes that the history of U.S. policy, especially the recent history, "is relevant to understanding what is being done today" (p. 9). In this respect, too, he agrees with Falk, but he goes on to say that he does not assume the benevolence of the U.S. government. "I do assume, however, that the easily predictable consequences of actions taken by the government were

7. In his famous poem, Rudyard Kipling describes the white man's "civilizing mission" among ungrateful, resistant "new-caught sullen peoples" as a thankless task, but one that must nonetheless be done since it is a moral imperative — hence the phrase "the white man's burden." Mahajan detects the same attitude of "enlightened paternalism" vis-à-vis peoples of the global South today. Writing in *The New York Times*, Michael Wines speaks about the "yawning gap between the West and much of the world on the value of a single human life" (Mahajan, *New Crusade*, pp. 99-100).

Dare We Speak of Hope?

in fact predicted by government planners, and that, therefore, the government is culpable and should be held accountable for them" (p. 9). And showing his understanding of the extraordinary role media play in a globalized world, he does not "ignore the facts just because they have been given little or no coverage" (p. 9).

Mahajan never mentions the word "megaterrorism," but it is clear that he knows that such a phenomenon exists. His approach, however, is different. He, too, sees the 9/11 attacks as a "crime against humanity," but he also sees it as a sign that the war America was waging outside its borders had "come home." "The main practitioner of attacks that either deliberately target civilians or are so indiscriminate that it makes no difference, is no shadowy Middle Eastern terrorist, but our own government. These attacks run the gamut from direct bombing, as the United States has done in Iraq (on numerous occasions), Serbia, Sudan, Afghanistan, and other countries in the past ten years alone, to denying people access to the basic necessities of life" (p. 9).

"If 'terrorism' is to be given an unbiased definition, it must involve the killing of non-combatants for political purposes, no matter who does it or what noble goals they proclaim" (p. 9). A whole range of authors have made the same point about these matters, citing U.S. foreign interventions over decades, causing the deaths of millions and the total destruction of infrastructure of whole countries.[8]

8. Cf. Noam Chomsky, *Year 501: The Conquest Continues* (Boston: South End Press, 1993). See also David Griffin on "the story of US imperialism" that would have to be told "against deeply entrenched mythology": US involvement in the overthrow of "constitutional governments such as Iran (1953), Guatemala (1954), Brazil (1961-64), the Dominican Republic (1965), Greece (1965 and 1967), Indonesia (1965-66), and Chile (1973), as well as interventions in Nicaragua and El Salvador." Griffin, "America's

Seen from this point of view, it is remarkable how much Falk's definition of megaterrorism is applicable to U.S. actions around the world; but in the context of his discussion of 9/11, he does not ask what severe consequences, symbolic or otherwise, those actions have had in those countries. From Africa to Indochina to Central America and Asia, people speak of the United States with fear and trembling or outright hostility, remembering the genocidal intent of U.S.-sponsored death squads, of successive proxy wars in the Congo, Angola, and Mozambique, and of military interventions because democratically elected governments threatened U.S. interests.

From the outset, America has spoken of its dominant role in the world in cosmic, visionary terms: "a world of empire, a world of our laws."[9] But what are we to make of America's plans for "Full Spectrum Dominance," which means not only being dominant on land, sea, and in the air, but having control of space — and naming one of the Space Command's programs "Rods from God"?[10]

Speaking in admiration of George W. Bush's insistence on "engaging *the world* in accordance with American principles," Lawrence F. Kaplan and William Kristol write:

The President also speaks bluntly of exporting the American creed "in keeping with our heritage and principles," which will in turn "create a balance of power that favors human

Non-Accidental, Non-Benign Empire," in David Ray Griffin, John B. Cobb, Richard A. Falk, and Catherine Keller, eds., *The American Empire and the Commonwealth of God: A Political, Economic, Religious Statement* (Louisville: Westminster John Knox, 2006), p. 5.

9. Cf. Ander Stephanson, *Manifest Destiny, American Expansion and the Empire of Right* (New York: Hill and Wang, 1995), p. 19, quoted in Griffin, "America's Non-Accidental, Non-Benign Empire," p. 8.

10. Griffin, "America's Non-Accidental, Non-Benign Empire," p. 13.

Dare We Speak of Hope?

freedom." By enshrining in official policy the tactic of military pre-emption, the objective of regime change and a vision of American power that is fully engaged and never apologetic, the Bush administration hopes to accomplish this happy end. We think it can.

With its untrammeled power, the United States could turn what up till then had been a failed policy in Iraq into a "model for success."[11]

To me, this sounds very much like Falk's visionary goals — unconditional motivation and tactical ingenuity all at once — except that no nation on earth can match the United States' tactical ingenuity or military strength. American Christian theologian Catherine Keller, who has earlier alerted us to the dangers of our language about God, writing on "omnipotence and pre-emption," is clear that "a theopolitics of omnipotence is clearly at work in American imperialism."[12] It is equally clear that the message of manifest destiny, American innocence and omnipotence, like the message of Osama bin Laden with many Muslims, seems to resonate with many Americans.

"Few would fail to notice the common ground between the perpetrators of 9/11 and the official response to it called 'the war on terror,'" says Mamdani:

Both sides deny the possibility of a middle ground, calling for a war to the finish. Both rally forces in the name of justice but understand justice as revenge. If the perpetrators of 9/11 refuse to distinguish between official America and the American

11. Lawrence F. Kaplan and William Kristol, *The War over Iraq: Saddam's Tyranny and America's Mission* (San Francisco: Encounter Books, 2003), p. viii-ix (italics in original).

12. Catherine Keller, "Omnipotence and Preemption," in Griffin et al., *American Empire*, p. 135.

people, target and victim, the "war on terror" has proceeded by dishing out collective punishment, with callous disregard for either "collateral damage" or legitimate grievances. Both practices are likely to nurture the spirit of revenge.[13]

By the time the second war against Iraq started in 2003, the peacetime bombing of Iraq had lasted longer (since 1990) than had the U.S. invasion of Vietnam or the war in Laos. Targeted sanctions, always pleaded for by the anti-apartheid movement as an alternative to violence, in Iraq "signified a truly novel and sinister development in the history of low-intensity conflict."[14] Instead of undermining the regime, it unleashed the mass murder of hundreds of thousands, mainly children.

Hearing this number (500,000) quoted to her in a television interview, Madeleine Albright, then secretary of state, responded to interviewer Lesley Stahl's question ("And you know, is the price worth it?") by saying, "I think it is a very hard choice, but the price — we think the price is worth it."

"That" says Rahul Mahajan, "is the philosophy of terrorism" — and I agree with him.[15] It is also a language so completely alien to the gospel as to be a strange tongue altogether. It is the language of idolatry.

---

13. Mamdani, *Good Muslim, Bad Muslim*, p. 230. Unconsciously, but seemingly naturally, President Obama seems to prove Mamdani's point in his Nobel Peace Prize speech: "Terrorism has long been a tactic, but modern technology allows a few small men with outsized rage to murder innocents on a horrific scale." See Barack Obama's acceptance speech: http:// www.msnbc.msn.com/od/34360743/ns/politics-white-house/t/full-text-obama's -nobel-peace-prize-speech (accessed Dec. 5, 2012). One could as easily apply this to America regarding the nuclear bombing of Hiroshima and Nagasaki, and America's ongoing war on terror.

14. Mamdani, *Good Muslim, Bad Muslim*, p. 186.

15. Mahajan, *New Crusade*, p. 10.

Dare We Speak of Hope?

The question is not only how we define terrorism, but also how, in these situations, do we as people of faith speak, believe, and act? What is the language of peace and hope for a world embroiled in endless war? How, especially, should Christians try to echo and emulate Jesus of Nazareth? The question is unavoidable. All sides try to justify war and sanctify violence in the name of God. Can Christian thinking, in the overwhelming vagueness that postmodern globalization has turned into a virtue, speak the clear language of salvation? Can we, as Erasmus of Rotterdam so fervently desired, seek the glory that is not steeped in blood?

The Morality of War Revisited

One consequence of the war on terror that is of great importance for theology and theological reflection is the return of the debate on the justification of war. It is an issue raised by President Obama himself in his Nobel Peace Prize acceptance address. In a globalized world, it is no longer possible to fully hide the consequences of war, even if that war is waged far away. Some aspects of it will always surface in some way. This might be covert or overt collusion between a government and mainstream media, and it happens regularly; but with a vigilant civil society and the clever use of social media networks, some of the truth gets to be heard somewhere, as the Arab Spring in the Middle East and North Africa has conclusively proved. Russian war crimes against the people of Chechnya, for example, could not be kept hidden, despite heavy official pressure on the Russian media. In the United States, the revelation of the U.S. conduct during its recent wars has raised to new levels the question whether those wars could be justified.

In Christian circles — Orthodox, Catholic, and all shades of

Protestants – the just-war tradition has come under renewed scrutiny. So fierce is the debate that one just-war defender speaks of the just-war tradition as facing a "frontal onslaught," of being "under siege."[16] I find this fact gratifying and encouraging. Progressive Christian thinking has not allowed itself to be totally overwhelmed and swallowed whole by the avalanche of right-wing Christian fundamentalism, however alarmingly that influence might have exerted itself on American Christianity and politics since the Reagan era. In the fascinating debate about the United States as imperial power and the consequences thereof for America and the rest of the world, progressive theological thinking in the North America has begun to reassert itself and is raising issues crucial for theological discussion, reflection, and action everywhere. The claim that America as a "Christian" country has God's special blessing and is thus always assured that whatever it is doing is done in God's name and with God's eternal blessing, is being exposed and resisted as seldom before.[17] Catherine Keller, taking us back to our reflections in the first chapter on the way we speak of God, is brutally honest in her appraisal of what she calls "American theopolitics":

> A theology of omnipotence electrifies the halo of American domination. Where then does the idolatry lie? In the fact that the United States plays God? Or, as I would put it, in the fact that it imitates a *false* God? Does the idolatry lie in our

16. Alexander F. C. Webster, "Justifiable War as a 'Lesser Good' in Eastern Orthodox Moral Tradition," *St. Vladimir's Theological Quarterly* 47, no. 1 (2003): 3.

17. For a progressive evangelical stance, see, e.g., Gregory A. Boyd, *The Myth of a Christian Nation: How the Quest for Political Power Is Destroying the Church* (Grand Rapids: Zondervan, 2005); Charles Marsh, *Wayward Christian Soldiers: Freeing the Gospel from Political Captivity* (New York: Oxford University Press, 2007).

emulation of a divine superpower? Or in our confusion of God with omnipotence in the first place?[18]

This is true, not just for America, but for all who seek to justify their lust for power and violence by calling upon God in this way. Another obvious reason for the current debate is the strange but deep-seated desire in Christian circles – with us for centuries now, from the Crusades to the wars on Iraq and Afghanistan to the slaughter by "The Lord's Army" in Uganda – to always try to justify violence and war as somehow an expression of the will of God. There is another reason, too. Defenders of international law find it difficult to justify U.S. actions in Iraq and Afghanistan – and the global war on terror generally, with its tragic outcomes in the actions of the state of Israel in the current siege of Gaza.

"In the present setting," writes Richard Falk, "it is dangerous in substance and as a precedent to validate the American claims against Afghanistan by reference to international law. . . . [There is] reason to prefer, or at least pay close attention to a just war rationale as, in effect, 'an exception' or supplement to international law."[19]

So here is the timely and important lesson for Christian theology: at a time when international law has been held up as the only binding standard for the conduct of states, secular or religious, and when the West itself no longer feels itself bound by rules based on religious argumentation, even staunch defenders of international law argue that in these new situations international law is somewhat inadequate (and subject to diverse interpretations in the United States and Europe) for the purposes of the justification of war in our times.[20] The Christian-based

18. Keller, "Omnipotence and Preemption," p. 134.
19. Falk, *The Great Terror War*, p. 123.
20. The lesson for us is here is important. In other areas of the struggle

just-war theory, because it "relies on generalized principles to help identify the dividing line between permissible and impermissible violence," is suddenly more helpful. Recourse to war is based on "the legitimacy of defensive force"; therefore, "just-war thinking, properly interpreted, can provide ample grounds for recourse to a just war. . . ."[21] So Falk opts for the Christian just-war tradition to justify war, even though he is emphatic that he speaks of the war against Afghanistan only. But is such justification able to stop there?

I make this point to highlight the grave responsibility of Christian thinking in the matter of war and peace. The perennial question "Is war ever morally justifiable?" has plagued Christians (and not just Christians) from the very beginning. The theory is important because it seeks not only to address the justness of the cause of war *(jus ad bellum)*; it also addresses the problem of the just means of war *(jus in bello)*. The agreed-upon rules seem to be the following:[22]

1. *Just cause:* The only morally legitimate reason for going to war is self-defense.

---

for justice, a "fall back" on conservative Christian ideologies is noticeable as well, e.g., in the area of gender justice and equality: "Many men are now actively resisting women's burgeoning demands for equal rights, and doing so increasingly through recourse to discourses of religious fundamentalism, not only Islamic, but also Christian and Jewish." See Stephen M. Whitehead and Frank J. Barrett, eds., *The Masculinities Reader* (Malden, MA: Polity Books, 2001), p. 7, quoted in Leandra Koenig-Visagie, "The Representation of Gender in the Afrikaans Corporate Church: A Fundamental Difference," in Juliana Claassens and Stella Viljoen, eds., *Sacred Selves: Essays on Gender, Religion, and Popular Culture* (Cape Town: Griffel, 2012), p. 181.

21. Falk, *The Great Terror War*, p. 124.

22. I follow the rules as set out in Holmes, *War and Christian Ethics*, pp. 4, 5.

Dare We Speak of Hope?

2. *Just intent:* The only morally legitimate goal in war is the restoration of peace, with justice for both friend and foe.
3. *Last resort:* War should be engaged in only when all other diplomatic paths fail.
4. *Lawful declaration:* Only lawful government has the right to initiate war.
5. *Immunity of noncombatants:* Those not engaged in war should be left unharmed.
6. *Limited objectives:* If the purpose of war is peace, then unconditional surrender is unwarranted, as is the destruction of the enemy's economy, infrastructure, or political institutions.
7. *Limited means:* Only sufficient force should be used to resist violence or restore peace.

In his argumentation, Falk names only four rules: the discriminating use of force (between civilian and military targets); proportionality (the relationship between responsibility, resistance, and capabilities of the target state); necessity (the attainment of military objectives and excessive force is to be avoided); and humanity (the upholding of humanitarian law and avoidance of human suffering).

While some have found the application of classic just-war theory enough in the present debate, others have gone further to attempt to use the just-war theory to also justify preemptive war, such as the United States regularly engages in. In my view, this very attempt, and the resistance to it from even fervent supporters of the tradition, underscores the deep dilemma the just-war theory presents us with. It attempts to justify war, but it has to go ever further, become ever more flexible, in order to create justifiability. Hence the inevitable abuse of language: war as "justice," an "act of love," "the supreme obedience and supreme sacrifice." Those more conscious of the weakness of human nature speak of war as "necessary evil," "lesser evil"; but those who find even these descriptions too negative, speak of war as "good, although a lesser good."[23]

"Christians who willingly and knowingly refuse to engage in a just war," writes Darryl Cole, "do a vicious thing: They fail to show love toward the neighbor as well as toward God."[24] And so the language of hope and life dies at the hands of the language of violence. The problem here is not just the abuse of biblical language that turns human revenge into love for God. It is the dilemma posed by war itself, the nature of violence and our human propensity toward it, our love for it, and our worship of it, as Walter Wink has warned. It is, even more precisely, the dilemma of the drawn sword. Once that sword is drawn, it has to be used, and once used, the use of it has to be justified. Ultimately, church historian John Ferguson is right:

> The arguments . . . are a replacement of the teaching of the New Testament by Greek philosophy or Roman law. There is nothing, literally nothing, distinctively Christian about the result. Yet these are the considerations which have dominated the majority of Christians for most of the history of the Church.[25]

23. See, e.g., the lengthy and highly emotional defense of "justifiable war as lesser good" by Webster, "Justifiable War," n40. He calls the growing resistance to the blanket moral justification of war in Orthodox circles "a spectacle," and goes far in trying to prove biblical justification for war. Those who disagree have fallen prey to a "contagion that knows no geographical or ecclesiastical bounds!"

24. As cited by Joseph Woodill, "Justifiable War: Response #1," *St. Vladimir's Theological Quarterly* 47, no. 1 (2003): 59.

25. John Ferguson, *War and Peace in the World's Religions* (New York: Oxford University Press, 1978), p. 103, quoted in Charles Kimball, *When Religion Becomes Evil* (San Francisco: HarperSanFrancisco, 2002), p. 161.

Dare We Speak of Hope?

The Dilemma of the Drawn Sword

The "drawn sword" I refer to here is taken from the title of an article by two American scholars reflecting on the fact that the U.S. government has decided to make preemptive war part of its foreign policy and the consequences of that decision for Christian thinking today.[26] But I do not mean only that. Neither do I mean the eagerness for war revealed in the notorious comment of President George W. Bush to his secretary of state, secretary of defense, and national adviser: "We have to have a war!"[27]

As I see it, in the United States at least, the sword was drawn the moment the decision was taken to make the militarization of the United States its top priority, making sure of success by spending more on this militarization program than all other countries in the world combined, despite simultaneously building up the biggest deficit of any country in the world. It is drawn the moment sentiments such these, uttered by *New York Post* columnist Steve Dunleavy, define public debate: "[K]ill the bastards. A gunshot between the eyes, blow them to smithereens, poison them if you have to. As for cities or countries that host these worms, bomb them into basketball courts."[28] It is drawn when a nation, in the words of American scholar Andrew Bace-

---

· 26. See David Clough and Brian Stiltner, "On the Importance of a Drawn Sword: Christian Thinking about Preemptive War — and Its Modern Outworking," *Journal of the Society of Christian Ethics* 27, no. 2 (2007): 253-71. Their attempt is to show that the just-war tradition cannot be used to justify preemptive war. Whether they actually believe that the argument can be made for "defensive war," or any war at all, is not clear. They recall the thoughts of Hugo Grotius as evidence against this usage, and they point to the political and moral pitfalls if such thinking should persist.

27. Mahajan, *New Crusade*, p. 105.

28. Quoted in Mahajan, *New Crusade*, p. 79.

vich, is "seduced by war,"[29] when, in its claim to be Christian, it disregards the words of Erasmus: "A good prince should never go to war at all unless, after trying every other means, he cannot possibly avoid it."

This is the difference between Augustine, Aquinas, Luther, and Calvin on the one hand, and Erasmus on the other. Those in the first category, unlike Erasmus, allow the sword to be drawn, and only then do they seek limitations to war even as they lament the sinfulness of human nature and the unavoidable excesses to which we are prone. But it all becomes pure justification. Erasmus pleads for such considerations *before* the sword is drawn, because he knows that if we were of this mind, "there would hardly ever be a war."[30]

This fundamental issue aside, I cannot see how modern warfare can possibly respond positively to the "rules of war" as envisioned even by the just-war theory; if "just cause" is to be replaced by preemptive war, and the hunger for "justice" becomes the equivalent of vengeance, as it was so vividly illustrated by the assassination of Osama bin Laden and the constant glorification of his death afterwards; and if diplomatic efforts can be so deliberately ignored and effectively undermined, as was the case with both the war on Iraq and on Afghanistan – then the criterion of "last resort" is rendered meaningless.

In a war as frighteningly comprehensive as the war on terror is proving to be, all the rest – "limited means," "limited objectives," and the upholding of humanitarian law in at least not targeting civilians – has become a cruel joke. John Breck warns: "With the lack of clarity that marks our motives, there

29. See Andrew J. Bacevich, *The New American Militarism: How Americans Are Seduced by War* (New York: Oxford University Press, 2005).
30. Erasmus, "On Beginning War," in Holmes, *War and Christian Ethics*, p. 177.

Dare We Speak of Hope?

is little chance we will wield our own weapons of mass destruction in a way that is either good or justifiable."[31] And he is right. Today's technology makes indiscriminate targeting almost inevitable: in the war against Serbia, for example, 70 percent of the "precision weapons" used, the so-called smart bombs, missed their military targets. One can hardly find a more apt description of the way the nature of war has changed than that of J. P. Sottile:

[We now must consider] a generation of future soldiers who've cut their canines on one shockingly graphic war stimulator after another. Just sitting there on a couch, pushing a button and killing one CGI enemy after another. Forget the push-ups; a ready-made army of push-button pilots awaits a near future filled with ultra-quick assassinations, all-too-easy bombing runs and the ominous and omnipresent patrolling of the skies.[32]

Disappointingly — and deeply so — not much has changed with the coming of Barack Obama as President of the United States.

"On [Obama's] watch," Tariq Ali says in the *Economist*, "American drones and special forces have been busier than ever, not only in Afghanistan and Pakistan, but also, it is reported, in Somalia and Yemen."[33]

31. John Breck, "Justifiable War: Lesser Good or Lesser Evil?" *St. Vladimir's Theological Quarterly* 47, no. 1 (2003): 98: "We have fallen into the trap of utilitarian expediency."

32. J. P. Sottile, "Boldly going where only drones have gone before," Reader Supported News: http://www.readersupportednews.org.opinion2/282 -98/7968 (accessed Sept. 19, 2011).

33. See Tariq Ali, *The Obama Syndrome: Surrender at Home, War Abroad* (London and New York: Verso, 2010), p. 69; see also Ali, "From Shoes to Soft Drinks to Underpants," *The Economist*, December 30, 2010. For the investi-

Even with President Obama's interpretation of the just-war theory as we have it in his Nobel Peace Prize speech, we cannot use the just-war theory as justification of the wars we fight today. This theory increasingly emphasizes the fact that those raising and defending it are not the soldiers in the field or those innocent men, women, and children who have nothing to do with the war or its probable – imagined or invented – causes. John Breck says that he expresses "the sentiment of countless dead, wounded and traumatized soldiers who have experienced for themselves what any form of military aggression is all about: 'God alone is good,' and 'war is hell.'"[34]

Resheathing the Sword

If we have a hopeful word to say at all, we should, in these matters, seek to be the voice of the innocent victims of war, never the voice of the powerful, who for whatever ambiguous reasons "have to have a war." As Charles Amjad-Ali reminds us, "As a Christian I say, *vox victimarum, vox Dei* – the cries of the victims are the voice of God."[35] I agree absolutely. The deliberate way in which the desire for war over the last decade or two has pushed aside international law and international solidarity should make us ever more determined to tirelessly work for effective international diplomacy based on justice and rights,

gative report on Yemen before the revolution of 2011, see Ali, *The Obama Syndrome*, Appendix 2, "A Note on Yemen," pp. 131-45. It gives no sign of foreseeing the Arab Spring and the revolution still continuing in Yemen; but the background material is highly instructive.

34. Breck, "Justifiable War," p. 98.

35. Charles Amjad-Ali, *Islamophobia or Restorative Justice: Tearing the Veil of Ignorance* (Johannesburg: Ditshwanelo Car'as, 2006), p. 156.

the upholding of international law and the recognition of the indispensability of multilateralism in international relations.

We must continue to encourage the search for nonviolent solutions to vexing problems – domestic as well as international – in politics, culture, or religion. But we must do more. We cannot any longer claim innocence in the understanding of the root causes of violence or of the consequences of political, social, and economic decisions because the innocence and the consequences happen to benefit us. This is the only way in which we can build that canopy of hope for the children of the world.

Besides, the moral dilemmas for ourselves have become painfully clear. T. Walter Herbert has persuasively argued that America's faith-based war in Iraq has only led to "catastrophic success." The price for what he calls "moral luxury, false innocence and denial of culpability," the costs of an imperialist Christian militarism, and the damage to America's moral fiber and standing, are simply too high.[36] When we kill hope in others whom we have turned into eternal enemies, we kill hope for ourselves as well. People of faith truly cannot be seen to seek to justify violence in any form whatsoever as a result of this proclaimed innocence. We are not innocent. We are the ones who throttle the chances for a redeemed future for the world. We must resolutely resist efforts to make religion a haven for extremism; we must resist the language that seeks glory in the shedding of blood and the destruction of life; and we must resist the violent, war-mongering fundamentalism that seeks to speak in the name of all religion. We must be firm: war is not an expression of the will of God, and it is not the way of Jesus of Nazareth.

36. See T. Walter Herbert, *Faith-based War: From 9/11 to Catastrophic Success in Iraq* (London: Equinox, 2009).

I am painfully aware that deeply complex situations might arise where nonviolent intervention comes too late, where the world, for various reasons, has hesitated too long, has erred fatally on the side of greed, neglect, or indifference, has invested too vastly and for too long in the entrenchment of tyrants of all kinds. Recent events in North Africa, Yemen, and Egypt offer such examples, as do those in Asia and the Middle East. In such situations, Christian solidarity cannot remain neutral, as if standing on the sidelines will relieve us of the moral obligations of love and justice, or as if the failures of the world's political elites absolve us from moral responsibility. There solidarity shall have to begin with the sharing of the pain, with our facing, and making, the same choices as the victims in that situation, together with them – however painful they may be.

Erasmus chastises those who, in their disappointment that they cannot find convincing justification for war in Scripture, claim the authority of the church fathers: "Even though Augustine approves of it and St. Bernard praises some soldiers, Christ himself and Peter everywhere teach the opposite. *Why is their authority less with us than that of Augustine or Bernard?*" And, as if he is speaking directly into the debates today, Erasmus, referring to the appeals to the church fathers, says, "Finally, if anyone will investigate the matter more carefully, he will find that no one has approved the kinds of wars in which we are now commonly involved."[37]

Christians have a sacred calling, not to justify but to prevent war, and to seek the things that make for peace, not just in local communities but among the nations. Globally, the spi-

---

37. See Holmes, *War and Christian Ethics*, p. 179 (italics added); see also Martin Luther King Jr., *Strength to Love* (Philadelphia: Fortress, 1963), p. 151: "The potential destructiveness of modern weapons totally rules out the possibility of war ever achieving a negative good."

ral of violence is sucking those who depend on it deeper into a quagmire from which there seems no escape. Tariq Ali writes:

> The world of "accidental" judgments and casual slaughter, the palimpsest that is the secret state, grew from World War II onward through the Cold War, and most recently, the "war on terror." Though coupled with the accrual of virtually unlimited executive power in the name of a continuous emergency that has lasted since Pearl Harbor, it yet failed to prevent the assault on the Pentagon and Twin Towers; meanwhile, it induced the visible state to approve torture, imprisonment without trial, the slow death of habeas corpus, the horrors of Guantánamo, Bagram, and Diego Garcia, until all these became as American as the once famous pie. So did the clichés justifying all this in the media. . . .[38]

But my opposition to violence and my pleas for nonviolence to become our first response as well as our last resort do not only come from observing the world and the devastation of global terror. They come from being in situations where violence has had no time to put on the mask of articulate self-justification. For myself – this much I have learned from Gandhi, Martin Luther King Jr., and the struggle in South Africa – I do not believe that violence in the long run can offer any lasting solutions. I am forever marked by what I have seen up close in my own country, done in the name of the Cause, for the sake of freedom and justice.

Like Albert Luthuli and Martin King, I remain deeply worried about the continuing and generational effects of internalized violence even on those who turn to it in a good cause, as they turn violence itself into a good cause. The violence of the

38. Ali, *The Obama Syndrome*, p. 116.

apartheid state was beyond measure, but in the time of my personal involvement in the struggle, black people – first through the philosophy of black consciousness and then in the work of the United Democratic Front – found a nonviolent way of responding to their oppressor's violence that reshaped the struggle since the 1960s and recaptured in powerful ways what was the ANC's undeniable legacy from 1912 to 1960, what Steve Biko called "the righteousness of our strength."[39]

In response to the first state of emergency, however, and in response to the merciless violent retaliation of the apartheid regime, we began to turn to violence and in the process turned the violence onto ourselves. In doing this, we also turned the violence *into* ourselves, allowing its pernicious presence to inhabit our minds and, unavoidably, our souls. We burned and looted, sacked and raged through the streets of our townships. We invented a horrific thing called the "necklace" (putting car tires around people's necks, pouring gasoline onto them, and setting them on fire). And we watched the victims burn to death. We executed them because we found out they worked for the apartheid security police (or we thought they did) and we called them "impimpis," a word that seemed to give us blanket authority to kill. We sometimes killed them simply because they disagreed with us, or were too afraid to take sides in our life-and-death struggle. We were convinced they had betrayed us. This never happened to whites, who were, in a very real sense, the real enemy.

Without thinking, or perhaps fully realizing it, we embraced the brutalization that apartheid had wreaked on us and made it our own. And then, as novelist Sindiwe Magona chastises us, we tried to hide those barbarous acts in innocent

39. Steve Biko, *I Write What I Like: A Selection of His Writings* (Johannesburg: Ravan Press, 1996), pp. 133-34.

Dare We Speak of Hope?

guises, "clothing satanic acts in innocent apparel."[40] We kept on talking about "the necklace"; we kept on calling those guilty of this deed "students" and "comrades." We gave no thought to our own dehumanization in the process, of what those acts would do to our souls, of what would become of us. In 1976, when we saw what the apartheid regime was willing to do in order to maintain white power and privilege – killing unarmed children – we lost our innocence. Now, however, what was threatened was our humanity, our own estrangement from the deepest being of African-ness: *ubuntu*.

It was in 1985, in an informal settlement called Lawaaikamp, near George in the Southern Cape, that I was personally confronted with the frightening possibility of seeing someone necklaced, someone who was accused of having "sold out" young activists to the police. The police had killed the activists, and we were gathered at their funeral. It took but a minute or so from the time the accusation was made to the moment the man was grabbed and dragged out of the church. By the time I emerged from the church, he was already bleeding from one eye, and someone had begun to pour petrol onto his head. When I intervened, the crowd mercifully spared his life; they, in turn, were spared of a burden too gruesome for their young shoulders to carry. But it was utterly stunning how swiftly the mood could change, the terrifying swing from singing hymns and freedom songs to shouting curses and plotting death.

Calling those moments back to mind, I understand better why South Africans in 2008, at the first signs of fear and feeling threatened by other nationals, took to the streets in mindless, xenophobic rage, burned and looted and with chilling noncha-

---

40. Sindiwe Magona, *Mother to Mother* (Cape Town: David Philip, 1998), quoted in Charles Villa-Vicencio, *Walk with Us and Listen: Political Reconciliation in Africa* (Cape Town: UCT Press, 2010), pp. 113-14.

lance once again brought back the "necklace." The shock of seeing the picture of a necklaced Zimbabwean in liberated South
Africa, our people singing and dancing in triumph around his
burning body, raises the question no South African should try
to avoid: What did we do when we clothed those acts in the
noble garments of "the struggle"? What did we do to ourselves
when we justified the perpetrators instead of admonishing
them, wrapped those acts in revolutionary pride instead of crying out in pain with the victims of our outrage?

My resistance to the embrace of violence is not based on a
theory of resistance and strategy only. It is based on the experience of the destruction violence visits on the souls of those
who, thinking they are serving a just cause, open the door to an
enemy beyond their comprehension and control.

Violence, I have written elsewhere, destroys the chances
for peace and reconciliation in the destruction of the other.[41] It
casts the other in the mold of an unchangeable, incontrovertible
enemy. It systematizes as well as personalizes enmity. After the
violent blow is struck, there are no more options left, and the
last word is already drowned in blood. Violence takes on a life of
its own as it feeds on ancient human emotions far stronger than
we realize, releases a relentless and deadly dynamic that we are
first not prone, then not able, to stop. It sweeps reason and better judgment aside as, in ritualistic helplessness that we do not
acknowledge to ourselves, we respond to the call of blood for
blood. Lifting the sword destroys the soul. Nonviolence appeals
to our other, better selves, to the truth we know about ourselves
as well as the other, but we too often deny: that in our crea-
turely, relational existence and our common humanity we are
not meant to be reduced to mere instruments of destruction,

41. See Allan Boesak, *Running with Horses: Reflections of an Accidental
Politician* (Cape Town: JoHo! Publications, 2009), pp. 112-13.

Dare We Speak of Hope?

that we are created to affirm, choose, and celebrate life rather than death. It kills the hope of the victims of our violence, and, as African-American pastor and public theologian J. Alfred Smith reminds us, "When hope dies, the pregnant mother of time dies with the unborn child of a redeemed future."[42]

Nonviolence affirms the humble acknowledgment of the possibility that we might be wrong, that the other is not just pure evil. It opens the way for the choosing of another path, to the *ubuntu*-fication of the other, because it longs for the affirmation of our humanity in the humanity of the other. Violence, in its irreversibility, is a reach too far for mortals such as us. Nonviolence acknowledges the existence of holy ground that we dare not tread on — such as taking the life of another. In this way, as we follow in the footsteps of Erasmus of Rotterdam, Christian faith affirms a way that does not seek glory in war and destruction, that is not steeped in blood or linked with the misfortune of others, nor brings us a victor who "weeps over a victory bought too dearly."[43]

We have more reason than ever to find a way to respond to Martin Luther King Jr.'s challenge: "The chain reaction of evil — hate begetting hate, wars producing more wars — must be broken, or we shall be plunged into the abyss of annihilation."[44] Indeed, we *must* learn to live together as brothers and sisters, or we shall perish together as fools. King pleaded with us that, even though "'the moving finger writes, and having writ moves on'. . . we still have a choice today: nonviolent co-existence or violent co-annihilation. . . . If we do not act, we shall surely be dragged down the long dark and shameful corridors of time

---

42. See J. Alfred Smith, "God's Invisible Hand," in Marvin A. Mc-Mickle, ed., *The Audacity of Faith*, p. 7.
43. See Holmes, *War and Christian Ethics*, p. 181.
44. King, *Strength to Love*, p. 53.

reserved for those who possess power without compassion, might without morality, and strength without sight. Now let us begin."[45] It is possible still for people of goodwill to build that canopy of hope and to work for a redeemed future for the people of the world.

45. Martin Luther King Jr., "A Time to Break Silence," in James M. Washington, ed., *A Testament of Hope: The Essential Writings of Martin Luther King, Jr.* (San Francisco: Harper and Row, 1986), p. 243.

CHAPTER FIVE

Dare We Speak of Hope?

Only If We Speak of Fragile Faith

"I borrowed a pen and paper from the pastor and began composing a letter. I wrote to a man who didn't exist yet, but who was someone I believed in with all my heart — our rescuer."

Immaculée Ilibagiza,
Rwandan holocaust survivor

"Our cries and our joys and our bewilderments — all those are taken up in this tremendous offering of our Lord and Savior Jesus Christ. . . . Nothing can be more hopeless than Good Friday; but then Sunday happens."

Desmond Tutu

"Strijdom, wathint' abafazi, wathint' imbokodo! Uzokufa!"

Song of the Women's March on the
Union Buildings, Pretoria, 1956

Killers Calling My Name

"I heard the killers call my name. They were on the other side of the wall, and less than an inch of plaster and wood separated us." With these words, Immaculée Ilibagiza begins her moving and fascinating book, *Left to Tell: Discovering God Amidst the Rwandan Holocaust.*[1] Immaculée is a Tutsi. In 1994 she was considered an enemy in her own country, a "cockroach," as the Hutu called them during that bloody and unforgettable tragedy. As she begins her book, she is in hiding, along with other equally terrified women and children, in a small bathroom in a pastor's house. The Rwandan conflict was becoming the Rwandan holocaust, "the most efficient mass killing since Hiroshima and Nagasaki," according to journalist Philip Gourevitch: more people were killed in a shorter period of time than the Jewish dead in the Nazi Holocaust.[2]

Her book makes devastating reading, revealing the mind-numbing depths to which human beings can sink in our inhumanity to each other; but it also tells of her amazing faith during all of her ordeals. The Rwandan horror story, however, goes far beyond the power-hungry dictators, the cold-blooded soldiers, the merciless mercenaries, and the bloodthirsty masses. It is about fragile faith and audacious hope. Simultaneously, the story is also about a preacher of the Word who shouts at soldiers: "What are you waiting for? Are you cowards? I bless this killing! I bless you for ridding this country of another cockroach!"[3] It is

1. Immaculée Ilibagiza, *Left to Tell: Discovering God Amidst the Rwandan Holocaust*, with Steve Erwin (Carlsbad, CA: Hay House Inc., 2006), p. xix.
2. See Philip Gourevitch, *We Wish to Inform You That Tomorrow We Will Be Killed with Our Families* (New York: Picador, 1998), p. 4; see also Jacques Pauw, *Dances with Devils: A Journalist's Search for Truth* (Cape Town: Zebra Press, 2006), pp. 65-124.
3. Immaculée tells of this incident as she recounts the killing of her

also about a "soft-spoken, fatherly figure," an "eminent bishop of the church" who provided guns to the soldiers to kill the Tutsi women and children who had gratefully taken refuge in the sanctuary of his church after he had lured them in with promises of protection. Then he stood by and watched as the soldiers he had alerted to their presence mowed them down. "That was the day," said Fr. Celestin Hategekimana of Rwanda afterwards, "when Satan wore a collar."[4] With one hand the bishop offered communion, and with the other he blessed guns and machetes. Speaking of the blood of Jesus, he waded ankle-deep in the blood of the innocent.

I cannot pretend to even begin to imagine what kind of shock such an experience must be to the human spirit, what havoc it wreaks on the soul, especially if you are a person of faith. The one moment you praise God for the one act of human kindness amidst the chaos and slaughter and bloodshed, thanking God for persons of faith with the courage to step into the breach for your sake. The next moment you are dragged out to die, not knowing which is the worst: the actual death, the monumental betrayal, or the powerlessness of God to stop it.

Fortunately, the pastor who hid Immaculée and her fellow refugees was not like that bishop. He offered real protection, and he risked his life doing so, giving true meaning to the words "human solidarity." It was while they were hiding in that small bathroom, all six of them in a narrow space with a toilet at one end and a cramped shower stall at the other — "there was no room for a sink," Immaculée remembers — the soldiers ransacking the house, calling her name over and over again, that she thought that, in the end, she too would die. She tried to pray, but could

---

brother, Damascene (*Left to Tell*, p. 154). Hereafter, page references to this work appear in parentheses within the text.

4. Pauw, *Dances with Devils*, p. 105.

not get farther than a trembling "Oh, God. . . ." She had no voice. "I had no saliva, and my mouth was drier than sand" (p. 130).

In that state of terror she dreamt about Jesus. Hovering above her and the others, Jesus spoke to her:

> Mountains are moved by faith, Immaculée, but if faith were easy, all the mountains would be gone. Trust in me, and know that I will never leave you. Trust in me, and have no more fear. Trust in me, and I will save you. I shall put my cross upon this door, and they will not reach you. Trust in me, and you shall live. (p. 131)

Then she jumped up and shouted at the others: "We're safe! Trust me . . . everything is going to be okay!" They looked at her as if she were mad. Indeed, it would be madness to take the word of someone who is as fearful and as weak as you are. But Immaculée Ilibagiza had discovered God amidst the terror and the fear and the threat of death. And when she discovered God, she discovered hope. When she discovered hope, she spoke life to her fearful companions: "We are safe," she told them. But they were not yet safe. There was still a long, long way between that bathroom and the certain taste of life. Even so, she had found her faith, and through her faith she found hope.

In hope they were saved that day, those women and children. Of course they could not see it yet — that safe, peaceful life. But "hope that is seen is not hope," the apostle teaches us. "For who hopes for what is seen? But if we hope for what we do not see, we wait for it with patience" (Rom. 8:24-25). It is only when we understand this that we acquire the power of conviction Paul shows at the end of that chapter: "What then are we to say about these things? If God is for us, who is against us? . . . No, in all these things we are more than conquerors through him who loved us" (Rom. 8:31, 37).

This hope in the unseen is what made Immaculée write a letter, against all odds, entirely foolish and laughable in the eyes of sober, reasonable, realistic people, to a man she did not even know existed, but believed that he did exist – and that she would meet him, their "rescuer." When she was cowering inside that little hiding place, she heard the soldiers outside the door speaking of her. "I have killed 399 cockroaches," said one. "Immaculée will make 400. It is a good number to kill" (p. xix). How does one react when killers speak your name? Her response was to write a letter.

This is how hope came to her, amid the voices shouting for her blood, in the shape of things not yet seen; but it was enough because it was grounded in her faith, and she gave life to hope – in a letter to a person who did not yet exist. This is what audacious hope is: a trembling hand writing words of fragile faith on borrowed paper while terror stalks on the other side of an inch of wood and plaster.

The Pitter-patter of Little Defeats

Years ago, a close friend of mine preached a great sermon with the wonderful title "The Pitter-patter of Little Defeats." She made the point that, as a church and as individuals, we are often done in, not by the huge losses in the big battles, but by the endless, small losses in the endless, small battles we seem to fight all the time. We are put down not by the overpowering might of the enemy, but by the small losses in those fights we expected to win: the pitter-patter of little defeats as we run down the hall toward the bedroom, where we try to hide and recuperate.

The worldwide Congregational Churches' Council on World Mission issued a statement on Christian mission in our world today. They call it a "statement of discontent." Somehow that statement reminds me of my friend's sermon. It speaks of hope as "that language of life, the *indomitable* and *audacious* conviction . . . that with God, all things are possible." I read the statement as based on the assumption that the words "indomitable" and "audacious" refer to our determination "not to settle for mediocrity or second best" only in the second instance. We cannot in the first place be speaking of ourselves, because even as we say it, we can hear the pitter-patter of those little defeats. We are not boasting here of our strength and our infallibility. Rather, we glory in the Lord, with whom "all things are possible."

"Indomitable" is a huge word to use about ourselves. It denotes an unwillingness to accept defeat, as the Oxford English Dictionary says, "even in a difficult situation." It is to be "very brave and determined" under all circumstances. But we are nowhere near always so indomitable. We fight and we suffer defeat; we lose battles on a daily basis. We are not invincible. We sometimes fight and run away, promising — and hoping — to fight another day. We start battles we do not finish because we run scared and buckle under pressure. I look around and, to my distress, I find that we are once again having to fight battles we thought we had won years ago. We have fought the battle against racism, and how we longed to speak truthfully about our "postracial" and "postapartheid" societies. But racism has returned in all its pernicious, public boldness, in all its subtle insidiousness, and it is as vicious and destructive as ever, and devastating in the inventiveness of its permutations.[5]

5. See, e.g., Michael Eric Dyson, *Debating Race with Michael Eric Dyson* (New York: Basic Civitas Books, 2007); see also Michelle Alexander, *The New Jim Crow: Mass Incarceration in the Age of Colorblindness* (New York: New Press, 2010); Paula S. Rothenberg, *Race, Class and Gender in the United States*, 8th ed. (New York: Worth Publications, 2010).

Dare We Speak of Hope?

We have engaged the evils of sexism and chauvinism, but patriarchy is everywhere, rampant in our public and our intimate spaces; it is solidified in our cultures, blessed by religion, justified by courts that pervert justice, and offered safe havens in our churches.

We stood up against the scourge and the folly of war, pointing to Hiroshima and Vietnam and Afghanistan and Ireland and Burundi. We prayed that the world would learn lessons from Hitler and the holocaust, and from the "catastrophic success" in Iraq.[6] But here we are, living in a world where our violence outstrips even our wildest imaginings of evil, albeit not our capacity for it. We are engulfed by megaterrorism carried out by stateless groups and states alike, the one as ruthless as the other. Just as we thought we had unlearned the words "nuclear bomb," we find that we have to learn the word "drones." What has remained constant are the words "death," "power," "destruction," "just cause," and "futile."

And still it is as it ever was: the glorifiers of war are the politicians who never see the blood but claim the glory. The need for war is for the profits of war, which go to the cowards in the board rooms, the makers of arms and the dealers in arms, for whom wars are always necessary. The casualties of war are the children and the women, the innocent whose war it never is. And, of course, the foot soldiers who, in the immortal words of Alfred Lord Tennyson, are never allowed to reason why — only called to do and die.[7] While the generals know what to do with their glory, the soldiers are at a loss at what to do with their anger and loss of humanity: "We are more angry at the generals

---

6. See T. Walter Herbert, *Faith-Based War: From 9/11 to Catastrophic Success in Iraq* (London and Oakville: Equinox Press, 2009).

7. See Alfred Lord Tennyson, "The Charge of the Light Brigade," in Hallam Lord Tennyson, ed., *Poems* (London: Macmillan, 1908), 2:369.

who are making these decisions and who never hit the ground, and who don't get shot at or have to look at the bloody bodies and the burnt-out bodies, and the dead babies and all that kinda stuff."[8]

In one single generation we have been taught to believe that war is the essential thing for the creation and survival of democracy. And even as we stand wonderingly by, a revitalized, truly frightening fundamentalism sweeps us aside, mesmerizing men and women alike with a package deal presented as blessings from God all wrapped into one: baptized capitalism, patriarchy, homophobia, bigotry, Christian patriotism, political power, religious exclusivism, and triumphalist war mongering – as Christian soldiers march on to Armageddon.

Even as we speak, the pitter-patter of little defeats becomes the thunderous footfalls of conquering legions.

As a church, our record in all of this is not good, I am afraid.

We are more concerned with building our own little fiefdoms than building the kingdom of God.
We are more comfortable with compromise than we are with authenticity and integrity.
We have so little credibility because we have so little to say that makes a difference.
We become irrelevant because we cling to words rather than build on deeds, and we forget Paul's admonition that "the kingdom of God depends not on talk, but on power" (1 Cor. 4:20).

8. Bob Graham, "I just pulled the trigger," *Evening Standard* (UK), June 19, 2003: http://www.eswheels.co.uk/news/articles/5402104. Quoted in Robert Jensen, *Citizens of the Empire: The Struggle to Claim Our Humanity* (San Francisco: City Lights Books, 2004), p. 34.

Dare We Speak of Hope?

We lose so many arguments because we are too self-assured and arrogant to learn anything new.

We do not have authority because we speak out of custom, not out of conviction.

We succumb to pressure because we have exchanged prophetic faithfulness for postmodernist lack of interest.

We hide behind the Bible, not seeing that it is the Bible that indicts us and declares us guilty.

We feel so powerless because we have lost our faith in the power of the Holy Spirit.

No, it is not of ourselves we speak when we use the word "indomitable." Not that we cannot be courageous, strong, and determined. We have all seen Christians who have stunned the world with their strength and courage, their endurance and determination, their patience and their faithfulness. They have glorified God, and they have empowered and inspired us all. We can be all that, because we *are* more than conquerors, but only "through him who loves us." We can be all that, if we live in prophetic faithfulness, do justice, love kindness, and walk humbly with our God.

It is not in ourselves that our strength lies, but it is in the conviction that with God all things are possible. It is the conviction that the struggle for justice, human dignity and worth, and the wholeness of the earth is not ours alone. We might lose a battle, but the conviction that with God all things are possible will survive, rise above defeat, make us brave beyond our weaknesses, strong beyond our fears.

Does it mean that we are never afraid, never doubtful, never anxious? Does it mean that, because we believe, we are always *sure?* Not if we understand the Bible correctly. During the days of our struggle, I have been fascinated and inspired by the story of Daniel's three friends in the fiery oven. During those excruciating

years I once preached on this text, a familiar story.[9] King Nebuchadnezzar has erected an enormous statue. Whoever would
not fall down and worship the statue representing the gods of
Babylon — and by the same token bow down before the king and
worship him as god — was to be thrown into a fiery furnace. However, three young Jews — Shadrach, Meshach, and Abednego —
refused to worship the statue. They would bow down to Yahweh
alone. About to be executed, they appear before the king, who
confirms the sentence: "If you do not worship," he tells them,
"you shall immediately be thrown into a furnace of blazing fire."
And then he asks the question that power, confronted with prophetic faithfulness, always asks: "And who is the god that will
deliver you out of my hands?" (Dan. 3:15).

This is followed by one of the most remarkable sentences
I know in the Bible. "If our God whom we serve is able to deliver us from the furnace of blazing fire and out of your hand, O
king, let him deliver us. But if not, be it known to you, O king,
that we will not serve your gods and we will not worship the
golden statue that you have set up" (Dan. 3:17).

"If our God . . ."? This comes as a shock. Is God not all-
powerful? Is not omnipotence one of the main attributes of
God? What about "With God all things are possible"? No wonder our Bible translators have such a problem with this verse.
For example, the New International Version reads: "If we are
thrown into the blazing furnace, the God we serve is able to save
us from it, and he will rescue us from your hand." Blessed assurance! Only afterwards comes the disclaimer, "But even if he
does not. . . ." The translation in my mother tongue, Afrikaans,
follows the language of the NIV: "Our God, in whom we believe,
can deliver us. . . ." The surety is right up front. That makes

9. See Allan Boesak, *Walking on Thorns: The Call to Christian Obedience*
(Geneva: WCC, 1984; Grand Rapids: Eerdmans, 1984), pp. 26-34.

Dare We Speak of Hope?

us feel better. That's more like it. That way, our certainty about God's supernatural intervention sounds a bit more humble, but still unshakeable. For us the risk is a mere formality.

But the text will not let us get away with that. The Aramaic, in which this part of the book of Daniel is written, leaves us no choice but to translate: "*If* our God, the one we serve, is able to save us. . . ." No walls of certitude to hide behind; no paved, illuminated path to walk on. If we walk, we walk by faith, not by sight. Sometimes our faith, like that of the three young Jews before Nebuchadnezzar, is full of *ifs*, *buts*, and *howevers*. And it is among those *ifs*, *buts*, and *howevers* that Hope stands up and calls to us. Hope means taking our chances with God.

But that is why our hope, like our conviction, is "audacious."

The Audacity to Hope

Most of us, when we hear the phrase "the audacity of hope," think about President Barack Obama's best-selling book of that title.[10] But the title is not original. Barack Obama first heard that phrase in church, listening to a sermon that Dr. Jeremiah Wright, God's prophet and his pastor, delivered in Trinity United Church of Christ in Chicago, where Obama met Jesus, was baptized, and accepted him as Lord.[11] But politicians do that all the time: take somebody else's ideas and sell them as their own.

10. Barack Obama, *The Audacity of Hope: Thoughts on Reclaiming the American Dream* (London: Canongate Publishers, 2006).

11. I am not the first or only one to notice this, of course. Curtiss Paul DeYoung takes note of this in his chapter entitled "When Prophets Are Silenced, Injustice Prevails," in Allan Aubrey Boesak and Curtiss Paul DeYoung, eds., *Radical Reconciliation: Beyond Political Pietism and Christian Quietism* (Maryknoll, NY: Orbis, 2012), pp. 115-29, 176n3.

Jeremiah Wright preached a sermon entitled "The Audacity to Hope." It is a brilliant, powerful sermon working with the story of Hannah in 1 Samuel 1. Jeremiah Wright tells us of a painting by the artist George Frederic Watts that he once studied as a student in humanities. It is, he says, a painting that seems at first glance to be a study in contradictions, because what is designated as the title of the painting and what is depicted on the canvas seem to be in direct opposition to each other. The painting is entitled *Hope*, and it shows a woman who is playing a harp and sitting on top of the world. She seems powerful and in control. But when you look at the painting more closely, "when the illusion of power starts giving way to the reality of pain," the world she is sitting on — our world — is one "torn by war, destroyed by hate, decimated by despair, and devastated by distrust." The world is, in fact, on the brink of destruction, and Watts, the artist, has contradicted the title, *Hope*, by depicting that despair on the canvas. Then one sees that the harpist is sitting in rags: her clothes are tattered as though she herself "[has] been a victim of Hiroshima or the Sharpeville massacre." When one examines her closely, one sees a bandage on her head, with blood beginning to seep through. Scars and cuts are visible on her face, arms, and legs, and the harp she is playing has all but one of its strings ripped out and dangling down. Even her instrument has been damaged by what she has been through, and she is more the classic example of quiet despair than anything else. Yet the artist dared to entitle this painting *Hope*. A seemingly hopeless contradiction.

Wright then speaks of the world in which we live, precisely the world depicted in the painting and the reason for the visage of the woman, linking it to the story of Hannah in 1 Samuel 1. The preacher talks about two dimensions in the picture: the horizontal dimension, hooking the woman to the world, and the vertical dimension, which we discover when we look above the woman's head. Above her head, some small notes of music move playfully and joyfully toward heaven. As we notice this, we begin to understand why the artist called the painting *Hope*. Jeremiah Wright preaches:

> See, in spite of being on a world torn by war; in spite of being on a world destroyed by hate; in spite of being on a world devastated by mistrust and decimated by disease; in spite of being on a world where famine and greed were uneasy bed partners; in spite of being on a world where apartheid and apathy fed the fires of racism; in spite of being on a world where nuclear nightmare draws closer with every second; in spite of being on a ticking time bomb with her clothes in rags, her body scarred, bruised, and bleeding, and her harp all but destroyed except for that one string that was left — in spite of all these things, the woman had the audacity to hope. She had the audacity to hope and to make music and praise God on the one string she had.

That one string was her connection to God. That's what Jeremiah Wright calls "the audacity to hope."

And in spite of the pain, he tells his congregation, in spite of the failures, in spite of the setbacks, the disappointments, and the heartache and suffering, we glory in tribulation because suffering produces endurance, and endurance produces character, and character produces hope, and hope never shames. So, no matter what the circumstances, we keep on singing the old slave spiritual: "There's a bright side somewhere. There's a bright side somewhere. Don't you rest until you find it. There's a bright side somewhere." It's not a question of what we see; it's a question of what we *don't yet* see. This preacher tells us, "Have the audacity to hope anyhow, no matter what you see!"[12]

12. Jeremiah Wright, "The Audacity to Hope," in Jini M. Kilgor, ed.,

It's no wonder Barack Obama could not resist the temptation. He just had to have that title. I don't blame him. But here's the thing: even though *The Audacity of Hope* is the title of his book, nowhere could I find a sustained discussion on the meaning of hope for him, not even an explanation of the title or a reference to Jeremiah Wright. Perhaps more importantly, no reference to justice for the hopeless. President Obama's campaign had identified hope "as a central virtue upon which he would hang his presidential administration," but when the White House doors closed behind him, he found it hard to speak of hope.[13] He dared not speak of hope because politics demanded that he spend more time on what New Testament scholar and black preacher William H. Myers calls "managing expectations" than on sustaining hope. The management of expectations is "an attempt to cap hope," Myers says, but at the same time "it is a slippery slope. . . ."[14]

In the book I am quoting from, *The Audacity of Faith: Christian Leaders Reflect on the Election of Barack Obama*, Christian

---

What Makes You So Strong? Sermons of Joy and Strength (Valley Forge, PA: Judson Press, 1993), pp. 97-109.

13. See Brad R. Braxton, "Hope in 3-D," in Marvin A. McMickle, ed., *The Audacity of Faith: Christian Leaders Reflect on the Election of Barack Obama* (Valley Forge, PA: Judson Press, 2009), p. 136. Braxton explains that hope has been the consistent element in black politics from Jesse Jackson to Barbara Jordan to Shirley Chisholm. "Hope serves as a bullet-proof jacket around freedom," says Braxton, "even when an assassin's bullet tried to kill freedom's dream at a Memphis motel in 1968. . . . Were it not for hope, this moment in history never would have happened" (p. 137).

14. William H. Myers, "A Hope That Does Not Disappoint: An Obama Presidency and Romans 5:5," in McMickle, *The Audacity of Faith*, pp. 77-92. See also Tony Campolo, "Hope Has Its Reasons," in McMickle, *The Audacity of Faith*, pp. 93-98: "What is right may not always be popular with the electorate. . . . [B]ut the church should proclaim to Barack Obama what biblical justice requires of him, even if its voice is not heeded" (p. 98).

Dare We Speak of Hope?

theologians speak as highly of Barack Obama as we South Africans did of Nelson Mandela. Obama is called a "politician-prophet," "possessed by the audacity of hope," and himself a "sign of hope."[15] Not all, but much of the language is pure euphoria, and as a South African, I understand that and do not judge it at all. But as we have learned in South Africa, euphoria is not hope, and politics and hope do not come seamlessly together; rather, they tend to confront each other. And it is a necessary, creative tension. But if they do blend — and that sometimes does happen — it can be a powerful and dynamic — though certainly dangerous — combination.

There is a reason why Mr. Obama could borrow the title, but could not sustain the promise of the title. There is a reason why, in the regretful words of William H. Willimon, who speaks of Obama as a "prophet/politician," the president could not "venture the full prophetic plunge into the countercultural, prophetic truth that God, not nations, rules the world and that all of us, even at our best, stand under the judgments of a righteous God whose ways are higher than our ways."[16] The reason, as Hebrew Bible scholar Walter Brueggemann has taught us, is as simple as it is sobering: "The task of prophetic ministry is to

15. Other publications run in the same vein; see, e.g., *From Beloved Community to Communities of Hope: A Small-Group Study Guide to Engaging Reconciliation* (Indianapolis: Christian Church [Disciples of Christ] Ministry of Reconciliation, 2009). As the title suggests, the booklet assumes a seamless progression from Martin Luther King Jr. to Barack Obama, and links the solution to the challenges awaiting him (the economic crisis, the war in Iraq and Afghanistan, the Israeli-Palestinian struggle, high and staggering unemployment, a poor education system, "and so much more") to Obama's faith in God as a "compelling component" in the president's character and to the fact that Obama "won on a platform of change and hope" (p. 16).

16. William H. Willimon, "Preacher-Prophet Obama," in McMickle, *The Audacity of Faith*, p. 86.

nurture, nourish, and evoke a consciousness and perception alternative to the consciousness and perception of the dominant culture around us."[17] While the prophetic consciousness aims to *dismantle* the dominant consciousness, that dominant consciousness is precisely the environment that politics craves in order to flourish, that it needs in order to gain legitimacy with the privileged and powerful.

This is not so much a critique of President Obama's policies as it is a critique of the nature of our politics everywhere, but especially the kind of politics needed to keep Mr. Obama in the White House, which seems to be the politics America wants most.[18] President Obama could not sustain the title of the book in his politics, because hope is simply too subversive of politics. Hope is patient but not pliable. Hope thrives in endurance, but it is the endurance of resistance, not of submission and compliance. Hope is sustained by what it does not yet see, but it is

17. Walter Brueggemann, *The Prophetic Imagination*, 2nd ed. (Minneapolis: Fortress, 2001), p. 3.

18. Social scientist and environmentalist/activist Paul Hawken contrasts the actions in 2007 of then President George W. Bush and of former President Bill Clinton. Hawken says that Bush "is on TV, snarled in a skein of untruths as he tries to keep the lid on a nightmarish war fed by inept and misguided ambition; simultaneously the Clinton Global Initiative (which is a nongovernmental organization) met in New York and raised $7.3 billion in three days to combat injustice, intolerance, and poverty." Of the two initiatives, "one of war and one of peace," Hawken asks: "Which addresses root causes? Which has momentum? Which does not offend the world?" (Paul Hawken, *Blessed Unrest: How the Largest Social Movement in History Is Restoring Grace, Justice, and Beauty to the World* [New York: Penguin, 2007], p. 4). But when Clinton was in the White House — and this is my point here — he waged war in Kosovo behind the highly suspect veil of "humanitarian intervention," ignored all the warning signs that pointed to the coming tragedy in Rwanda, and allowed American sanctions to destroy Iraq's infrastructure. Not even the death of more than 500,000 Iraqi children who could not get medical treatment could move him.

Dare We Speak of Hope?

enraged at what it does see. When politicians speak of hope, it is political pietism for the sake of expediency. When prophets speak of hope, it is prophetic iconoclasm for the sake of justice. When politicians speak of hope, it is with the certitude of power. But when prophets speak of hope, it is with the vulnerability of faith.

When Mr. Obama first heard Rev. Wright's sermon, it was about hope despite the devastation of the world. Politics cannot speak this language because politics causes the very destruction that hope critiques and resists. The world depicted in the picture is a world of hunger, disease, and poverty. While politics looks for ways to police poverty, hope looks for ways to eradicate poverty. Our politics will not end poverty, even though we possess the scientific know-how, the material means, and the economic possibilities — and even though the eradication of poverty is now a moral imperative. All we lack is the political will.[19] Politicians are too indebted to those who have too much to be persuaded by those who have so little. The consequences of hope are too radical for politics: justice, equality, mercy, kindness, love, peace, remorse, forgiveness, conversion, transformation, walking humbly with God, seeing the world through the eyes of those who suffer rather than through the eyes of the powerful and privileged. Politics has no word for it.

The realism of politics cannot abide the realism of hope. Political realism demands the "management of expectations."

19. World Game Institute, 1997: As of 1997, $19 billion was spent worldwide on weapons every week. See also the United Nations Development Report, 1997 (New York: United Nations, 1997): $80 million would grant access to clean water, social services, and basic education for the world's poor for ten years; this equals the financial assets of the world's seven richest men (these figures cited in Joanna Macy and Molly Young Brown, eds., *Coming Back to Life: Practices to Reconnect Our Lives, Our World* (Gabriola Island, Canada: New Society Publishers, 1998), p. 16.

But in every political dispensation, the management of expectations applies only to the poor and powerless. In every other way, politics rushes to fulfill the expectations of the rich and powerful no matter how unrealistic — in real terms — those might be: from instigating and waging war, to granting mining licenses in eco-sensitive areas, to issuing permits for logging in the rain forests, from deregulating the restless making of money and privatizing the people's resources to bailing out highly irresponsible banks and lowering the taxes on the wealthy.

The expectations of the poor — of a redistribution of resources; of decent housing, decent jobs, and decent pay; of proper education, safe neighborhoods, and clean streets; of service delivery and honest, uncorrupted government — those expectations are always too high and have to be "managed," in other words, toned down. The realism of hope challenges and confronts the realism of *Realpolitik* because it requires the fulfillment of *God's* expectations: "Let justice roll down like waters, and righteousness like an ever-flowing stream," thereby exposing the "realism" of politics as the sham it really is.[20]

20. As an example, Paul Hawken points out the disastrous effects when World Bank policies were imposed on the fishing industry in Tanzania. Nile perch were introduced into Lake Victoria, a ravenous predator that eliminated 350 varieties of the lake's native fish. Today, flash-frozen perch fillets are exported to Europe via massive Ilyushin cargo planes which return, sometimes with flour and dried peas for refugees, sometimes with arms and munitions that support Central Africa's refugee-creating wars. The native population does not benefit from this $400 million industry. Having lost most of their traditional fisheries, they rely for food on the fish heads and scraps thrown away by the fish processors. "What poor people experience when market reforms and other fiats sweep through their barrios or squatter settlements is . . . a far remove from what World Bank bureaucrats imagine in their pristine offices in Washington, D.C.," drawing up their plans to square with the "realism" of market demands (see Paul Hawken, *Blessed Unrest*, 129-30).

Dare We Speak of Hope?

Hope seeks to *celebrate* justice; politics seeks to *domesticate* justice. Hope and justice belong inextricably together. The hope that the nations put in Jesus the Messiah, Matthew's Gospel reminds us, is the hope in the Servant of Yahweh, who will proclaim justice to the Gentiles, who will not rest, and who will refuse to be crushed until he has brought justice and hope to the nations, with the whole earth rejoicing. Politics has no words for that.

In politics, "audacity" means unbridled power, military strength, economic ruthlessness, boundless arrogance, reckless manipulation, brutal might, and violation with impunity. In hope, "audacity" is steadfastness in faith, endurance in suffering, outrage at injustice, solidarity in struggle, courage in pain, love despite hatred, celebrating the unseen as though already seen, walking humbly with God, and glorying in the faith that "with God all things are possible."

In politics, "audacity" is the hallmark of the powerful; in hope, "audacity" is how the powerless gird on strength. Politics has no words for that. That is why the politician dares not let go of the hand of the prophet. And that is why only prophetic truth can turn politics into the holy calling it is meant to be.

Hope, Resurrection, and the Women

If hope is the presence of comfort at the cross, as we have argued, then hope is the presence of triumph at the grave. Throughout history, black people have wrestled with the meaning of the cross, the presence of evil, and the sense of suffering.[21] In the

21. See, e.g., James Cone, *God of the Oppressed* (Maryknoll, NY: Orbis, 1997); see also Cone, *The Cross and the Lynching Tree* (Maryknoll, NY: Orbis, 2012). For womanist views on suffering and evil, see Emilie Townes, ed., *A Troubling in My Soul: Womanist Perspectives on Evil and Suffering* (Maryknoll, NY: Orbis, 1993).

1970s, black South African theologian Manas Buthelezi spoke of black people's whole lives being "one, long Good Friday."[22] Easter is almost unreal then, a pietistic escapism into something that falls "outside the sphere of experience of the average black Christian who takes concrete life seriously," says theologian Tokatso Mofokeng. Easter remains "a vague and illusive scriptural information and article of the apostolic faith." In fact, following Jesus and his history "ends in paralysis on the cross at Golgotha."[23] No, says Desmond Tutu:

> Our cries and our joys and our bewilderments — all of those are taken up in this tremendous offering of our Lord Jesus Christ. . . . Nothing can be more hopeless than Good Friday; but then Sunday happens.[24]

Desmond Tutu is right, and it is not escapism, as Mofokeng fears. There is no pretense that the "long Good Friday" does not exist, no attempt to deny our "bewilderments and cries" and the *mysterium iniquitatis*, the overwhelming mystery of evil that the violence on the cross represents and that a life of oppression, degradation, and dehumanization becomes. What Tutu is already seeing, though — and already rejoicing in — is the "joy" of the truth that after Good Friday, "Sunday happens."

Good Friday is not endless. Hope is present at the cross, and she emerges from the grave, witnessing to the power and empowering the reality of the resurrection. The resurrection of Christ is God's insurrection, God's rebellion, for that is the

22. Manas Buthelezi, "Violence and the Cross in South Africa," *Journal of Theology for Southern Africa* (December 1979): 52.

23. Tokatso Mofokeng, *The Crucified Among the Cross-bearers: Towards a Black Christology* (Kampen: Kok, 1983), pp. 28, 29.

24. Cited in Jim Wallis and Joyce Hollyday, eds., *Crucible of Fire: The Church Confronts Apartheid* (Maryknoll, NY: Orbis, 1987), p. 69.

meaning of the Greek word the New Testament uses: God's *apanastasia* against all sin, inhumanity, death, and destruction. It is God's uprising against the violence that nailed Jesus to the cross and freezes us into paralysis. It is God's rebellion against our resignation, our need to compromise with evil, and our tendency toward despair and hopelessness, against our willingness to sell the dream of God for God's people to the highest bidder in the name of "realism."

In faith, we walk hand in hand with hope from the open tomb into the waiting world.

> The open tomb is the surest guarantee against the enclosure of our soul, against the imprisonment of our spirit, against the interment of our hopes which, if they remain in the grave of our lost-ness, will surely and irrevocably be lost. The emptiness of the grave is the divine reversal of the emptiness of human history, re-creating it from a space of hopeless helplessness to the arena of God's life-giving power. To be raised with Jesus is to join God in that revolt against the forces of evil, whoever they may be and in whatever guise they may appear.[25]

So this is where Hope brings us, hand in hand with God in God's revolt against the forces of evil that seek to destroy God's world, and hand in hand with Jesus, who is God's revolution against the powers and principalities, and who is moving toward the saving transformation of the world. It is that revolution that we join when we stand with God.

In 1956, when the apartheid regime decided to extend the hated "pass laws" to black women, twenty thousand angry, cou-

---

25. See Allan Boesak, *The Tenderness of Conscience: African Renaissance and the Spirituality of Politics* (Stellenbosch: Sun Press, 2005), p. 129.

rageous, hope-filled women marched on Pretoria. They knew the pass laws meant the further destruction of black family life, even stricter control of movement for black people, and enforced acceptance of the Bantustans. It meant giving up all hope of democracy, of rights, of dignity, and of any sense of belonging in the country of their birth. They refused to accept that. So they marched to the Union Buildings, the offices of Prime Minister J. G. Strijdom, black women and white women, a glorious expression — amid apartheid's bigotry and racial separation — of the rainbow nation not yet seen but hoped for and acted out in visionary anticipation of freedom. Together they challenged and confronted the awesome might of the apartheid state.

They marched and they sang: *Strijdom, wathint' abafazi, wathint' imbokodo! Uzokufa!* ("Strijdom, you have touched the women; you have struck a rock! You will be crushed!").[26] The women sang of freedom, they sang of defiance, and they sang of hope. They did not come to kill him, but they saw with prophetic clarity — as they announced that his time had come — that his regime would not last, that apartheid would be crushed, that for South Africa's oppressed people, life was waiting.

In that song they brought it all together: the anger against a racist system that sought to destroy their humanity; the courage to rise up and fight against injustice and oppression; the refusal to accept suffering as the will of God for their lives and to let evil have the last word; the faith that with God *all* things are possible.

In the eyes of the world, these women were weak; but in reality they were strong, because they had righteous anger, and courage, and faith. They were strong because they saw beyond

26. For information on the history of this march, the reader can access, among others: http://encyclopedia2.thefreedictionary.com/South+Africa+women%27s+Day.

apartheid, because they marched apartheid into the dust. They were strong because they hoped apartheid into nothingness. Like the women at the open tomb that first resurrection morning, they believed that the "long Good Friday" must come to an end, because they saw beyond the crucifixion and believed the resurrection. That march was their *apanastasia*, their revolt against the overwhelming realities of apartheid to embrace the promise of struggle and a new humanity. They rose up against the ideologues of apartheid and dared to reimagine South Africa. In politics, imagining is too often the kiss of death. In faith, imagining is a life-giving force.

All around them there was still the darkness and hopelessness of apartheid, but they sang, and they knew intuitively with the African slaves in America, that "there's a bright side somewhere . . . don't you rest until you find it; there's a bright side somewhere." "Strijdom, you have touched the women, you have struck a rock!"

Hope not only gives us a song; Hope gives us a harp. The world those South African women challenged may have been in chaos, controlled as it was by the powers of domination and oppression. Their bodies may have been bruised and battered and wounded. Their harps may have been broken, left with only one string. But on that one string they made music to the glory of the God of love, freedom, and hope. They sang light from darkness, hope from hopelessness, life from lifelessness. They sang and danced us to the well from which generations are still drinking. They changed the world.

CHAPTER SIX

Dare We Speak of Hope?

Only If We Speak of Dreaming

"We cannot help but believe that the old hatreds shall some-day pass; that the lines of tribe shall soon dissolve; that as the world grows smaller, our common humanity shall reveal itself; and that America must play its role in ushering in a new era of peace."

Barack Obama, 2008

"As I sit in Qunu and grow as ancient as its hills, I will continue to entertain the hope that there has emerged a cadre of leaders in my own country and region, on my continent and in the world, which will not allow that any should be denied their freedom, as we were; that any should be turned into refugees, as we were; that any should be condemned to go hungry, as we were; that any should be stripped of their human dignity, as we were."

Nelson Mandela

"Dreams are, by their very nature, an affront to the status quo. Dreams are God's way of calling us to holy discontent with things as they are. Dreams urge us on to righteousness and restlessness with the world as we know it. Dreams are the subtle songs of the soul that echo the vast distance between who we are and who we, by the grace of God, might become."

Raphael Warnock

Hoping Is Dreaming

Hoping is dreaming, and it is remarkable how often our capacity to hope is linked to our capacity to dream. We dream of the things we hope for, and we hope that our dreams might become reality. It is remarkable, too, how often the hope that hopeful politics engender is linked to our dreams of justice, peace, and equity. The wellspring of our dreams is the fountain of our hopes. For this reason the election of President Obama is frequently mentioned in the same breath with Martin Luther King's dream of a different America.[1] Robin L. Smith takes that one step further: "But a dreamer is identified," she writes, "as in the stories of Joseph in the book of Genesis, Dr. King and President Obama."[2] Certainly for African-American Christians,

---

1. See, e.g., Robin L. Smith, "Dreaming Like a Fool," in Marvin A. Mc-Mickle, ed., *The Audacity of Faith: Christian Leaders Reflect on the Election of Barack Obama* (Valley Forge, PA: Judson Press, 2009), pp. 20-24; Gina M. Stewart, "Almost But Not Quite," in McMickle, *The Audacity of Faith*, pp. 46-51; Raphael Warnock, "Dreams from Our Fathers," in McMickle, *The Audacity of Faith*, pp. 64-69; and William H. Willimon, "Preacher-Prophet Obama," in McMickle, *The Audacity of Faith*. Willimon speaks of Obama as "the prophet (who) dares to dream" (p. 83).

2. Smith, "Dreaming Like a Fool," p. 23.

who have deep, vivid, and enduring memories of and roots in the civil rights struggle, that is a completely natural reach. In the sermon from which our third epigraph for this chapter is taken, Raphael Warnock thanks God that America now has a "dreamer in chief" sitting in the Oval Office. "The fact is," Warnock says," freedom would never have come to fulfillment and Barack Obama as president never would have been possible were it not for the one who dared challenge the conscience of the nation with four simple words: 'I have a dream.'"[3]

Again, as a South African who knows about the stony road and the bitter, chastening rod, who knows about singing a song full of the hope that the present has brought us, who treasures the bonds between our two struggles – now become global struggles – I feel the deep resonance of this connection. But from our own experiences and from my reading and understanding of the Bible, I bring with me a critical hesitation.

In the reflections on President Obama's election in the book *The Audacity of Faith*, there is also such a critical hesitation. Speaking of the powerful moment of Obama's inauguration, Gina M. Stewart reminds us that, while it is important not to minimize the significance of what transpired on January 20, 2008, "it is also important to resist the temptation to declare that King's dream has been fulfilled."[4] Reflecting on the same inauguration address, William H. Willimon observes: "Even as I write this, our new president has ordered a massive surge in the troops in Afghanistan, determined to bring that unruly nation in line with our righteous purposes." Willimon is troubled by what he discerns as "the rather conventional upbeat American call to arms and optimistic swagger of America as the hope of the world." Bringing his reflections to a close, Willimon

3. Warnock, "Dreams from Our Fathers," p. 65.
4. Stewart, "Almost But Not Quite," p. 47.

wishes "that our new president had ventured the full prophetic plunge into the countercultural prophetic truth that God, not nations, rules the world. . . ."[5]

I have already ventured, in the preceding chapter, some thoughts on that "prophetic plunge into countercultural truth." Suffice it to say now that Barack Obama's dream is perhaps more embedded in American civil religious discourse than in the biblical story of Joseph's dream.[6] On this issue he seems less aware of the countercultural truth than is theologian Frank A. Thomas, who observes that "when we define the American Dream singularly in terms of economic benefit, a better, richer, and happier life for all is not possible without domination and exploitation of subjected people. What we need is a reconceptualization of the American Dream, to, in the words of Langston Hughes, 'bring back our mighty dream again.'"[7]

Preaching from Martin Luther King Jr.'s pulpit in historic Ebenezer Baptist Church in Atlanta, Raphael Warnock, speaking about Obama, reflects on the story of Joseph, "that blessed biblical prototype of a dreamer," lying on his deathbed and still daring to hope and dream: "I am about to die, but God will surely come to you and bring you up out of this land to the land that he swore to Abraham, to Isaac, and to Jacob. . . . When God comes to you, you shall carry up my bones from here" (Gen. 50:24-25).

It might be helpful to ponder these words and their mean-

5. Willimon, "Preacher-Prophet Obama," pp. 85, 86.

6. See Valerie Elverton Dixon, "Barack Obama and the American Civil Religion," in McMickle, *The Audacity of Faith*, pp. 105-10.

7. Frank A. Thomas, *American Dream 2.0: A Christian Way Out of the Great Recession* (Nashville: Abingdon, 2012), p. xiii. Thomas says: "I believe that the key to the fulfillment, expansion and reclamation of the American Dream lies in the discourse of subjugated people, for whom the American Dream was/is unfulfilled" (p. 114).

ing at the close of our reflections on hope. In doing this we shall keep in mind Warnock's very apt observation, which serves as a guiding word to our final chapter: "Dreams are, by their very nature, an affront to the status quo . . . God's way of calling us to holy discontent with things as they are . . . [urging] us to righteousness and restlessness with the world as we know it." We have pondered the nature of our politics and how hard it is for politics to speak of hope with integrity without a profound transformation of the nature of our politics. We should sound the same caution here. If dreams are "holy discontent" with the way things are, then politician-dreamers should make that discontent the heart of their politics, the central plank in their platform, the driving force behind the policies they put in place. The "affront" to the politics of the status quo lies not in the dreaming of dreams, but in the audacity to make those dreams a political reality. Politician-dreamers should be ready to accept the consequences of that affront to the status quo.

Hence we must take seriously Warnock's admonition: "But it takes a tough mind and a tender heart to hold on to hope. It takes audacity to dream and to believe. It takes faith and courage and tenacity to see visions and dream dreams."[8] This is a toughness and a tenderness of a different kind than politics is used to. Our politics thinks of toughness as a resoluteness to keep the world the way it is, since the world as it is, is so profitable for the privileged and powerful. This toughness calls for a determination to transform the world so that it conforms to the dream of God for God's world. It is a tenderness that shuns the sentimentality and romanticism of political pietism and sees the world through the eyes not of the powerful, but of the powerless and the suffering.

8. Warnock, "Dreams from Our Fathers," p. 65.

This restlessness is the commitment to walk humbly with God, which means, as I have written elsewhere,

> to stand where God stands, and to fight for whom God fights: the poor, the weak, the powerless and the defenseless. It is to have the courage to know that trepidation before the might of the powerful is overturned by the fear of the Lord. It is to understand, without doubt or equivocation, that justice is what Yahweh requires. Not seeks or asks, or hopes to eventually coax from our unwilling hearts, but *requires*.[9]

Restlessness with the world as it is and willingness to affront the status quo is the restlessness of Hope's two daughters, as we have heard from Saint Augustine. But why is it an affront? It is an affront because it dares to contaminate *Realpolitik* with the dreams and hopes of the poor, the powerless, and the afflicted. It is the contamination that Jesus embraced when, in the matchless words of the Christ Hymn, which Paul clings to as he faces the might of the empire, "he emptied himself, taking the form of a slave, being born in human likeness. And being found in human form, he humbled himself and became obedient to the point of death — even death on a cross" (Phil. 2:7-8). Paul writes this to a people already living under the reign of terror that Rome was, "having no hope and without God in the world" (Eph. 2:12). They have to learn to see that the power of the Messiah is realized in a different way from the power of Rome. Christ's *doxa* is a totally different glory from that of the caesar. The way to that glory is different; the way in which it is achieved is different; the quality thereof is different. But it

9. See Allan Aubrey Boesak, *The Tenderness of Conscience: African Renaissance and the Spirituality of Politics* (Stellenbosch: Sun Media, 2005), p. 234.

is nonetheless a concrete, political alternative to the politics of every empire, ancient or modern.[10]

God reveals that it is in this Jesus, the one who has "emptied himself," taking the form of a slave, identifying with the humiliation and the pain of slaves, allowing himself to be contaminated by their lowliness — it is in this love to the very end that God has entered into the human story, demonstrating true majesty. For precisely "in the form of a slave" is Jesus "very God." The slave is Lord, the name "every tongue shall confess," and before whom "every knee shall bow," is the name of the contaminated one, because he takes upon himself the suffering of God's afflicted children and God's contaminated cosmos. And *as such* he challenges the powers and principalities who reign with injustice, and he brings them openly to shame (Col. 2:15). It does indeed take a tough mind and a tender heart to understand this — and to make it the heart of one's politics. This is the urge toward righteousness and restlessness that the dream creates. It calls for prophetic politics of a kind that politicians tend to back away from; but it is exactly the kind of politics that the world needs and that prophetic faithfulness should insist on.

Joseph the Dreamer

We know Joseph as "the dreamer" from the captivating story in Genesis 37. There Joseph, the second youngest of twelve brothers and one sister, is painted as Jacob's favorite, mostly because he is the firstborn of Rachel, the wife Jacob loves (Gen. 29:18, 30). Rachel's sister, Leah, Jacob's first wife, remains unloved

10. See G. H. ter Schegget, *De Andere Mogelijkheid* (Baarn, The Netherlands: Ten Have, 1973), pp. 44-45; Boesak, *The Tenderness of Conscience*, p. 99.

(Gen. 29:31). Joseph is introduced as the dreamer who dreams that his family bows down in obeisance to him. His dreams infuriate his brothers (make them "hate him even more") because the dreams indicate that he will have "dominion" over them (Gen. 37:5). The brothers first aim to kill Joseph, but they end up selling him as a slave to a passing caravan after Reuben, the eldest, has intervened.

Reflecting on Joseph the dreamer, we should be mindful that there are two mistakes we might be likely to make. The first is to think that Genesis 37 was *Joseph's* dream; the second is to think that Genesis 37 was Joseph's *only* dream. Joseph, having landed in Egypt and having earned the favor of the pharaoh, likely interpreted these dreams as dreams of his own greatness, and in truth, his spectacular rise in the palace and the empire might have given him reason to believe that this was indeed so. But as Robin Smith rightly reminds us, "God gives dreams and visions to men and women that the world might be healed, not to massage the ego of any individual, family, or political dynasty."[11]

Indeed, Joseph's dream in Genesis 37 was not a dream about power, status, wealth, or position — despite how Joseph himself might have (mis)understood it. In reality it was a dream about serving humankind, about solidarity and justice, about keeping humanity and humanness alive in the world. That is why the dream was not Joseph's dream. It was God's dream. In the end, the high point of the dream, the fulfillment of the dream, is not the distance of the throne but the embrace of reconciliation; not power, but servanthood; not lording it over others, but liberating others; not the power to bring death, but the gift to foster and treasure life. In the end, the deepest meaning of the dream is not being a king, but a brother. The moment Jo-

11. Smith, "Dreaming Like a Fool," p. 20.

seph thinks the dream is his dream — and about his power — things go horribly wrong.

It is instructive to see how the dream is threatened by the ebb and flow of Joseph's life. First comes the alienation from his brothers, to such an extent that they "hated" him. "They could not speak peaceably with him," is the weighty expression used in Genesis 37:4. Because it was no longer possible to speak peace with him, they could not live in peace with him. The narrative moves with startling swiftness. By verse 11, the hatred and enmity are compounded with "jealousy"; and it is clear, by the time we reach verse 19, that the reader should not be surprised: "Here comes this dreamer." It is not the light, teasing tone older brothers will sometimes adopt in friendly family bantering. The disdain drips from the words. Joseph has long since ceased to be a brother. He is "this dreamer" whose dreams stir hatred and fear, and soon it will become clear that this is no laughing matter.

The conclusion is the deadly logic of estrangement and peacelessness: "Come now, let us kill him." By the time we come to the end of the verse, the conspiracy is thought out, welded and justified in their minds and hearts, and ready to be executed. The deepest motivation is simple and, among the brothers, undisputed: "And we shall see what will become of his dreams." Throwing him in the pit after he is dead, or selling him as a slave — it doesn't matter. As long as they are rid of him. The tearing into shreds of that special multicolored robe ("with the long sleeves") is a metaphor for the shredding of the human and familial relationships that the brothers have really accomplished.

Second, the dream is threatened in Potiphar's home, just when Joseph thinks he is establishing himself in this new land, earning the trust of his master, becoming successful as he helps Potiphar to "prosper" (Gen. 39). In spite of all that — perhaps because of it — Potiphar's wife accuses him of attempted rape, and his protestations of innocence make no difference. Just as

Potiphar's wife has stripped Joseph of his garment, Potiphar himself strips Joseph of his honor, his position in the household, and his hopes and dreams for the future. An enraged Potiphar sends Joseph to prison, where the third assault on the dream occurs. I speak of assault not simply because Joseph is in jail, for even there Yahweh does not desert him, in fact "shows him steadfast love" (39:21). Joseph finds favor in the eyes of the prison warden, and consequently it goes as well as one could expect in a prison. But prison is a dreamless place; it is not the place in which dreams can be fulfilled.

In prison it is not Joseph but the two disgraced officers of the Pharaoh's court, his cupbearer and the court baker, who dream. It speaks volumes for Joseph's sensitivity that he is not so consumed by his own situation, by the unfairness of his imprisonment, by bitterness at the injustice of it all, that he does not notice the troubled faces of his fellow prisoners. "Why are your faces downcast today?" he asks them. Then they tell him about their dreams, and Joseph the dreamer becomes Joseph the interpreter of dreams. The interpretation is favorable for only one of them: the cupbearer will be restored to his position, but the baker will be hanged.

Joseph wants no reward from the grateful cupbearer, but he does ask a favor loaded with his own hope-filled longings for justice and, deeper still, for the fulfillment of his own dreams. "Remember me when it is well with you; please do me the kindness to make mention of me to Pharaoh, and so get me out of this place" (Gen. 40:14). Joseph knows and reminds himself that, however satisfactory his life in prison might be, he is innocent of the crimes he was accused of, his imprisonment is unjust, and he does not belong in prison. His life and the fulfillment of dreams still await him – but outside "this place." No matter how well they treat him in prison, this is not a place to be. Here are the stirrings of that restlessness the dreamers of dreams carry within themselves: a longing for justice and the steadfast knowledge that what outsiders consider a good life in prison is still no life at all, because it is not a place of hope. Nor is it a place for dreams.

Genesis 40 ends on a sobering, if not chilling, note: "Yet" — in other words, despite Joseph's help and solidarity in prison, despite the enormous change in his life, despite the fact that he knows of Joseph's innocence, and despite his own promises — "the chief cupbearer did not remember Joseph." The narrator piles one verb on the other to demonstrate that injustice is piled on injustice: ". . . but forgot him" (40:23). So Joseph remains in prison "two whole years." The dream is threatened by injustice done and hope shattered.

For two whole years Joseph does not dream. Instead, it is the pharaoh who dreams, and at last the cupbearer remembers. At least he has the decency to remember his sins as he remembers Joseph: "I remember my faults today." He recalls Joseph, speaks to Pharaoh, and Joseph is taken out of prison. Once again Yahweh is with him, and Pharaoh recognizes Joseph as one in whom the Spirit of God dwells (Gen. 41:38).

After his interpretation of Pharaoh's dreams, Joseph's rise in the palace is no less than spectacular. He becomes Pharaoh's second in command, with all of Egypt ordered under him, except for Pharaoh himself. Four times in ten verses the narrator tells us that Joseph ruled "all of Egypt." "Bow the knee!" the heralds who run before him shout as Joseph's chariot roams the streets (Gen. 41:43), and no one in all of Egypt could "lift up hand or foot" without Joseph's consent (41:44). Joseph's name was changed to Zaphenath-paneah, a powerful name that means "the god spoke: he shall live."[12] Married to the daughter

12. See Claus Westermann, *Genesis 37–50: A Commentary* (London: SPCK, 1986), p. 96.

of a priest of On, he was thereby brought into Egypt's nobility and became a true prince of Egypt (41:45). The NRSV translates 41:40 this way: "And all my people shall order themselves as you command." The literal translation, however, is closer to the meaning of Joseph's transformation and the power now given to him: "And on your mouth all my people shall kiss you."[13]

In 1 Kings 19, Yahweh consoles and encourages a deeply troubled Elijah by assuring him that he is not alone, as he claims, but that there are "seven thousand in Israel . . . all the knees that have not bowed to Baal, and every mouth that has not kissed him" (19:18). The kiss on the mouth is the recognition of divinity; it has the connotation of worship. Joseph is to be kissed on the mouth as a sign that the people shall be unquestioningly obedient to his every word. Joseph, it seems, is much more than just "prime minister" of Egypt. He now has the status of a god.

When the Dream Flees

Joseph runs an extremely efficient administration and makes a name for himself. The wisdom of the interpreter of dreams is now employed for the fulfillment of Pharaoh's politics. When he is finished, Egypt has so much grain stored away that "it [is] beyond measure" (41:49). His sons are born, and Joseph names the firstborn Manasseh, for, he says, "God has made me forget all my hardship and all my father's house." He mentions his hardships and his family in one breath: he is over both, as done with the one as he is with the other. Just a little earlier, Joseph had wanted desperately to be remembered, and in prison

13. See also Victor P. Hamilton, *The Book of Genesis, Chapters 18-50* (Grand Rapids: Eerdmans, 1995), p. 504.

he could still recall that he was from another country, where there was family. Now he just wants to forget. His second son he names Ephraim, a living reminder of his success in Egypt (41:52). His roots are now here, and he is firmly planted; the land of his misfortunes has now become the land of his power. It truly seems as though Joseph's dream has been fulfilled. And it is meaningful that Joseph now acts as if the fulfillment of his dream is the same as the fulfillment of Pharaoh's dream. His bond with the empire has now become inextricable.

On this point Walter Brueggemann writes, "The hidden way of the dream outflanks both the power and the wisdom of the empire." However, if the dream was first threatened by external forces, the dream will now be threatened by Joseph himself, and his commitment to the empire. Brueggemann's reflections position Joseph over against the empire, and that is absolutely correct — up to a certain point. But Joseph has now become a son of the empire. "He is fully Egyptian," Brueggemann says.[14] However, I read that in a more ominous sense. From his position of power, Joseph runs famine-ridden Egypt like a hard-nosed business mogul. Six times in verses 54-57, the word "famine" is mentioned: the gravity of the situation cannot be overestimated. Egypt and Canaan "languish" in hunger (v. 13). The word "languish" appears nowhere else, and it seems to connote the people "being stunned" by the ferocity of it.[15] When the hunger that has devoured the world strikes even the Egyptians, Joseph "open[s] up all the storehouses and [sells] to the Egyptians" (41:56).[16] There are some commentators who

14. Walter Brueggemann, *Genesis*, Interpretation series, James Luther Mays, gen. ed. (Atlanta: John Knox, 1982), p. 334.
15. See Lowenthal, *The Joseph Narrative in Genesis: An Interpretation* (New York: KTAV Publishing House, 1973), p. 125.
16. See Robert E. Longacre, *Joseph: A Story of Divine Providence* (Winona Lake: Eisenbrauns, 1989), p. 255; A. van Selms, *Genesis Deel II: De*

read this text to mean that Joseph, in typical, welcoming generosity, opens the grain storehouses to "give away" the grain.[17] But he doesn't: he *sells* it to the people.

But where did he get all that grain in the first place? From the very people who had worked the land, planted and harvested, and had to give it up to Pharaoh in tribute and taxes. It was for this very reason that Joseph had so thoroughly scoured the land (41:46). Joseph now makes those very same people pay for the food they had produced (Gen. 41:46-49). The rich and powerful, the privileged elite who live in the shadow of the palace, may still have enough. But the impoverished masses fall on hard times very quickly. It is they who "[cry] out to Pharaoh for bread" (Gen. 41:55). The people cry out to Pharaoh, but it is Joseph in his newfound power that they have to face.

"If there is one portion of Genesis that could as well have been left out without causing a vacuum, it is this piece," writes Hebrew Bible scholar A. van Selms, referring to Genesis 47:13-26.[18] We would not have missed it, he means to say, and its absence would have caused no gap in the flow of the narrative. Eugene F. Roop calls it an "anecdote," yet "one senses that much of the history of the use and abuse of power is mirrored [here]."[19] Still, it is inserted here for a reason – and a very important one, in my view. Claus Westermann sees this as an addition from

<hr />

Prediking van het Oude Testament (Nijkerk, Netherlands: Uitgeverij Callenbach NV, 1967): "The NBG [Dutch Bible Society translation] correctly reads *wayyašbēr*: Joseph does not buy for, but sells to the Egyptians what they need" (p. 216).

17. See, e.g., Lowenthal, *The Joseph Narrative in Genesis*, pp. 125-26. Lowenthal argues that Joseph's plans target only the wealthy; he actually does what he does "to help the poor" (p. 126).

18. Van Selms, *Genesis Deel II*, p. 261.

19. See Eugene F. Roop, *Genesis*, Believer's Church Bible Commentary series (Scottsdale, PA: Herald Press, 1987), p. 281.

some author who was "impressed" with Joseph's administrative skills.[20] But I see this addition as intended to critique Joseph's use of power, to illustrate the stark contrast between Joseph the dreamer and Joseph, prince of Egypt. It is added to show the historical consequences of the use and abuse of power.[21] Even here the prophetic strain in the Bible asserts itself, countering the dominant, uncritical imperial narrative, offering an alternative understanding of God's will for the people.

After the interlude about Joseph's family, Genesis 47:13 again picks up the mantra that has run like a virus through the text: "Now there was no food in all the land, for the famine was very severe." The Joseph we meet now is not the brother who is moved to tears by the presence of his family, the one who weeps "on the neck of Benjamin." The one we meet in Genesis 47 is Zaphenath-paneah, the son of the empire. Some suggest that the name must not have been important, for it is mentioned only once. I think the true significance of that name does not lie in the number of times it is mentioned, but in the awareness of alienated otherness that it awakens in Joseph and thus brings to the text, and in the contrast it denotes between Joseph the dreamer and Joseph the prince. The Egyptian name is not mentioned here: it is not necessary because Joseph's behavior recalls the name. The writer of the story believes we need to know about the way Joseph exploits the dire economic situation of the people to benefit his master, the pharaoh. There are painful but crucial lessons to be learned here. The word "food" (bread) is crucial here: it is the people's deepest need, and it is this need that Joseph most ruthlessly exploits.

20. See Westermann, *Genesis 37-50*, p. 176.
21. I agree with Roop, who says, "In a double twist to the story, Joseph has established an economic order that would subsequently enslave his own people" (*Genesis*, p. 281).

Joseph "collected all the money": it means the small amounts of treasured belongings, nuggets of gold and silver, precious stones in people's private possessions — all their savings. All these are now gathered in the treasure chests of the palace, over which Joseph has control (Genesis 47:14). In this way all possession of precious metals large and small is now in Pharaoh's hands. Joseph uses the famine and the hunger of the people to drive a hard — and heartless — bargain. "Give us food!" the Egyptians plead with Joseph. "Why should we die before your eyes?" (v. 15) When all their money is gone, Joseph takes the next step: "Give me your livestock, and I will give you food in exchange . . ." (v. 16).

The narrator quite intentionally spares us no detail: "So they brought all their livestock . . . the horses, the flocks, the herds, and the donkeys" (v. 17). Their whole means of living and survival was now gone, gathered into Pharaoh's wealth. And it does not end there. The following year, as the famine worsens, the people are forced to return. "The herds of cattle are now [all] my lord's," they say. "There is nothing left in the sight of my lord but our bodies and our lands." There is something deeply moving in the words "We cannot hide it from you." They place themselves completely at the mercy of those with the power to save their lives, not with confidence but in pathetic desperation. The peasants understand that they are now at the end of the road. Their lands — their last means of survival, independence, and dignity — and their bodies are all that is left. They are offering themselves in slavery to Pharaoh. "We with our land will become slaves to Pharaoh; just give us seed, so that we may live and not die, and that the land may not become desolate" (vv. 18-19). If they have hoped for some compassion, they had come to the wrong person. Joseph follows the cold and calculated logic of the empire: "So Joseph bought all the land of Egypt for Pharaoh. All the Egyptians sold their fields. . . ." As for the people, "he made slaves of them, from one end of Egypt to the other" (vv. 20-21).

Joseph's ruthlessness here is stunning. The one who protested that he was unjustly sold into slavery, who knows the pain, suffering, and humiliation of slavery, now becomes the enslaver, the owner of slaves. In ancient agrarian society, the person or family with no land has no future. Joseph's actions place a generational curse on the poor. Losing their lands means losing the last bit of independence, their last shred of dignity, their last hope for a future. The best they can hope for now is to become workers for the wealthy class in the cities, while their lands generate income for the powerful and privileged. Is there a suggestion of a "forced removal" here?[22] The luckier ones are ordered to stay and work their former lands for Pharaoh: "Then Joseph said to the people: 'Now that I have this day bought you and your land for Pharaoh, here is seed for you: sow the land'" (Gen. 47:23). The land will belong to the Pharaoh, and they will pay tribute, but at least they will have food for their families — "for your little ones," Joseph says (v. 24).

The usual rate on borrowed land was 20 percent. However, these lands were not "borrowed"; they were appropriated. Moreover, Joseph taxes them not on the "borrowed" portion of land, but on the harvest, which was much more.[23] The emergency measures of the seven lean years have now been made perma-

---

22. Robert Davidson seems to think so (see his *Genesis 12-50*, Cambridge Bible Commentary on the New English Bible series [Cambridge: Cambridge University Press, 1979], pp. 287-88), and I agree. "Forced removals" brings to mind horrific images and vivid memories for black South Africans during colonial and apartheid times, from which we have not yet recovered, as they must for Palestinians today because of the policies of the state of Israel, the illegal occupation of Palestinian land, and the traumatic effects of the "Wall of Separation."

23. Van Selms, *Genesis Deel II*, p. 263.

nent law. The pain and suffering of the poor is turned into gain for the powerful. The disaster of the famine is turned into permanent shock and awe for the poor and powerless. What for a brief moment sounded like compassion ("you and your little ones") quickly turns about to be just another turn of shrewdness for the sake of profits. And here is the tragic internalization of oppression: so utterly relieved are they just to be allowed to survive that, even though they have lost everything, they turn to Joseph with the pathetic gratitude of the truly conquered: "You have saved our lives; may it please my lord, we will be slaves to Pharaoh" (v. 25), a sentence that vibrates with humiliation. Joseph does all this "for Pharaoh." On this point the Masoretic text meaningfully reads: "For Pharaoh, for the stomach."[24] This is the absolute pit of hopelessness.

Does it tell us anything at all that in this whole passage the name of Yahweh is not mentioned even once? Earlier the writer could not tell us enough how Yahweh "was with Joseph." That divine presence kept the dream alive. When the name of Yahweh is not mentioned, the dream is no longer mentioned. In the face of such exploitation and injustice, of such naked abuse of power, of such hardness in the face of suffering, the dream flees.

The Dreamer Returns

If this piece had been left out of the biblical narrative, as van Selms observes, the likelihood is that we would have (re)discov-

---

24. Van Selms, *Genesis Deel II*, p. 263, observes: "Perhaps they thought of the fable of Menenius Agrippa, in which the ruling classes are described as the stomach of the body of the state." See also 1 Cor. 12:12-27. In either case, it graphically denotes the insatiable greed of the ruling elites and their abuse of power to satisfy it. Over against this greed is the hunger of the people for both food and justice.

ered the dream when we (re)discovered Joseph. I am speaking of the Joseph of chapters 42-46, the Joseph who is at first hard on his brothers, but then dissolves into tears of contrition, reconciliation, and joy. And, honestly speaking, this is the Joseph we love, the Joseph of the dream, for he is the Joseph of *our* dreams.

Here the son of the empire rediscovers who he is: the son of Jacob, the brother of his brothers. "I am your brother Joseph" (Gen. 45:4). We should read this sentence as though it has three exclamation points at the end. He adds, ". . . whom you sold to Egypt" — not as another reproach to heighten their guilt but as evidence of the authenticity of his claim. He has to say that because his brothers truly do not recognize him. It is not because he now sits on a throne and wears Egyptian royal robes, I think. Rather, it is his demeanor that they do not recognize. His *spirit* has changed. He no longer has the spirit of a son of Israel; he has the spirit of an Egyptian prince. His invitation to them to "come closer to me" is about much more than the respectful, fearful distance they keep from the throne. It is about the distance that lovelessness and peacelessness create. What Joseph wanted so intensely to "forget," in chapter 41, he now remembers — not for revenge or to gloat, but in understanding: "So it was not you who sent me here, but God . . ." (v. 8). The scenes in Genesis 45 are dramatic and deeply transformational, certainly for Joseph and his brothers, but also for every reader of this story ever since.

The amazing thing is that the Bible itself does not want us to stop there, thus the insertion of that discomforting, disturbing piece about Joseph and his politics of power. As moving as the reconciliation between Joseph and his brothers is in Genesis 45, it is clearly not enough. For that reason the narrator, after yet another interlude (Gen. 47:27-50:14), returns to the uncompleted reconciliation, and with that to the point of the Genesis 50 story, Joseph's second dream.

That second dream is not possible until the reconciliation is complete. In Genesis 50, it becomes clear that the brothers are not yet free of their guilt, and neither is Joseph. The brothers are not sure whether the assurances given (in Gen. 45:1-15) will hold. They seem unsure whether or not they are still dealing with the Egyptian in Joseph. The brothers, in pleading for forgiveness once more, "fall down," precisely as Joseph dreamed as a seventeen-year-old lad. But is that the fulfillment of the dream at last? Most commentators, including Brueggemann, seem to think so: "The dream is now unwittingly fulfilled by the brothers."[25] The conclusive verse here seems to be Genesis 50:20 (NIrV): "You planned to harm me. But God planned it for good." In my view, however, those are not the words that seal the reconciliation.

What makes the reconciliation genuine, radical, and durable — and what brings the real fulfillment of the first dream — is not verse 20, but verse 19: "Do not be afraid! *Am I in the place of God?*" That is the key sentence here. Those are not the words of a powerful ruler spoken from his throne of power. Those are the words of one who has rediscovered the God of the dream. The demigod of Egypt, without whose say-so "no one could move hand or foot in all of Egypt," who had power over life and death, and who used that power to enslave the peasants of Egypt and strip them of all that mattered, now knows how utterly sinful it was to behave as if he were indeed "in the place of God." Only now is his life an open book, and he can read it, not because he is the son of the gods, but because he is a child of God. Now he knows that God did not "plan" all this for the sake of power and its abuse over the lives of helpless and powerless peasants and for the enrichment of the empire, but for flourishing, hope, and meaningful life for the most vulnerable.

25. Brueggemann, *Genesis*, p. 371.

The dreamer does not return until the reconciliation is complete, as I have argued above. That is true, but perhaps even that is not enough said. The dreamer really returns only after Joseph lets go of the empire and its seduction of power and embraces instead the power of the dream. Only then is space created for the second dream, and that dream becomes the embodiment of Israel's hopes. "The last words of Joseph are neither reminiscences nor grudges. *They are hopes*," Brueggemann says emphatically, and he is right. "It is the last, best hope of Joseph."[26] And hope comes to him as in a dream: "I am about to die; but God will surely come to you, and bring you up out of this land to the land that he swore to Abraham, to Isaac, and to Jacob. . . . When God comes to you, you shall carry up my bones from here" (Gen. 50:24-25). With these words Joseph turns his back on the power of the empire and embraces the dreams of the powerless. His power will not realize the dream, but the power of the God of the slaves will. There will come a pharaoh "who did not know Joseph," but the God of the powerless will "know" their sufferings and their dreams of freedom.

Now Joseph knows that, though he is "honored" in Egypt, and shares power with the mighty pharaoh — and despite the name he gave his son — Egypt is, after all, not his home or his destiny. The dream is not about power over others, it is about servanthood; it is not about enslavement, but about liberation; it is not about death, but about life. It is not about revenge for the past, but about sharing hope for the future. It is truly not about Egypt, but about the Promised Land. It does not matter that Joseph is on his deathbed, that he will never see the fulfillment of this dream. What matters is the dream, not the fulfillment of it in his lifetime. And Joseph *knows*. So the narrator explicitly makes the point: when Joseph dies, he is embalmed

26. Brueggemann, *Genesis*, p. 379 (italics in original).

Dare We Speak of Hope?

"and placed in a coffin in Egypt"; but he is not buried in Egypt (50:26). His life may end there, but the dream does not. That is how the book of Genesis ends: open-ended, with its face toward the future filled with hope. There would still come a pharaoh "who did not know Joseph," there would be 400 years of slavery and pain and suffering, but Joseph already saw the day when Yahweh would "come down" to save God's people (Exod. 3:8).

Throughout the narrative, the narrator makes the point: the brothers "go down" to Egypt to get food, and so Jacob must "go down" to see his son again. Life may seem "up," but in reality it is a descent. Egypt may be a land of plenty now, a land of power, but for Israel's children, it will become a dismal place. The power that Joseph enjoyed here will be turned against his people. Now Joseph knows that God's "coming down" is the true salvation: to bring God's people "up" from Egypt. There is a different power at work here, entirely different from the kind of power he came to know in Egypt and had embraced. This is the act of liberation that brings true life, and it comes not from the gods of Egypt, who smiled "life" upon him, but from the God of slaves, of the downtrodden, and of the wronged. Likewise, he wants his bones to be "carried up." The whole line of thinking is "up," "away from here." This place might still be a place of power and might and plenty, but one day it will be a place of enslavement and pain, and his hope is vested in the faith that he will be taken "away from here." This is the dream that allows Joseph to see beyond the empire and its allures. It goes against the status quo, even one that now seems to benefit Joseph.

Dreaming, Hope, and Politics

As Nelson Mandela sat in his birthplace, Qunu in the Eastern Cape in South Africa, growing old as its ancient hills, he dreamed dreams for his country, his continent, and the world. Just as with Joseph, in Walter Brueggemann's words, those dreams were neither reminiscences nor grudges; they were *hopes* — hopes for South Africa, the African continent, and for the world. Mandela hoped for and dreamed of freedom, which is not a grandiose idea or a magnificent ideal. Freedom represents the simple needs of God's little people: to live in peace in their own homes, to not go hungry, to have dignity. Their dreams are of having dignity, worth, security, and peace, and of belonging — to be at home, surely, but to be at home in the country of one's birth and in a world in which justice and peace have found a home. Mandela turned his mind not to the grandiloquent speeches of those the world considers great. He turned to the simple dreams of those whom the world does not regard, those of unimpressive proportions, who have no strength — or permission — to speak, but whose wounds speak for them. In doing this, he reminded us that the shape of a just world lies in the fulfillment of the hopes of the poor and powerless, the silenced and the downtrodden, not the elites whose wealth has flourished beyond their wildest dreams, even as they trample on the dreams of the poor.

Mandela may have been the revered "father of the nation," the first democratically elected president of a free South Africa; and he may have seen the dawn after the long night of oppression, and he did indeed see power wrested from the hands of the apartheid oppressor. But with clarity of mind and integrity of heart, he knew that his people are not yet free from hunger, from fear, from the indignity of an unfulfilled life. At the end of his life, he had no more time for the exaggerated claims, false loyalties, and blind obeisance that party politics requires; rather, he saw his nation and the world through the eyes of those whose suffering has still not ended. As he sat in Qunu, he really did not want for anything. He had been one of those given power far beyond his wildest dreams. But he looked at the world not from his place of secured glory, but as a hope-filled captive of *ubuntu*: my humanity, and my human well-being, is caught up in your humanity. I cannot be what I want to be until you are what you need to be. The fulfillment of my dreams is measured by the contentment of your lives. So he dreamed, even though his dream might be an affront to those who so fervently claim his name in the creation of a "new South Africa."

As he grew old, he did not look back in self-satisfaction. He did not wallow in – or claim merit for – his suffering, those twenty-seven years he needlessly spent in prison. He did not bemoan the fact that his eyes grew weak because of the dust of the stones he was forced to break on Robben Island. He did not coddle the grudges he may have rightfully held: the countless humiliations that come with imprisonment, the many years he missed his family, the passage of the unforgiving years that made him an old man when he finally regained his freedom. He did not curse apartheid's cruel rulers, who forced him into a choice for violence when all peaceful efforts were crushed; nor did he vent his anger at the white judges in apartheid's courts that condemned him as a terrorist when he fought for the freedom of his people. He knew that the masses who love him suffered with him and on his behalf every step of that long walk to freedom.

He did not regret the fact that he offered white South Africans forgiveness, even if it now looks as if they did not all deserve it. He did not retract his magnanimity in the face of their unrepentant intractability. His love remained constant for *all* his people. Mandela did not indulge in reminiscences: how the world saw in him an icon of the struggles of all freedom-loving people; how they once made him into a demigod who could do no wrong; how he was admired as the greatest statesman of our times. He knew that the time had come for greater, purer things. As he grew ancient as Qunu's hills, he did not narrow his look toward his birthplace or his country or his own people, as old people are allowed to do. There was a wideness in his gaze that took in all the world as he hoped for freedom — from fear, from hunger, from indignity — for all God's children in the whole of God's world.

Despite the disappointments and bewilderments that any long life brings, he did not give up on politics; rather, he hoped that the politics of justice might become not just the hope of the people, but the guiding light of those who hold power entrusted to them by the poor. He hoped for "a cadre of leaders" who will work for freedom, security, and justice, and he spoke of these in simple, human terms: freedom, refugees, hunger, and dignity. As he spoke, he remembered in the only way that is authentic: ". . . as *we* were."

The words "as we were" are a reminder that it is the people's hopes that matter and that will bring hope to our politics. Mandela knew that inasmuch as it is possible to speak of a South African miracle, that miracle did not fall out of thin air, nor was it the calculated outcome of those highly praised secret negotiations, the triumphal tally of a clever endgame; it was, in a real sense, the fruit of struggle, and suffering, and sacrifice. It was the fruit of faith, as I have observed elsewhere, "sometimes wavering, always under attack, but never diminished, of a believing people who in sacrificial love, amazing endurance, and a God-given gift for forgiveness, refused to give up hope. They recognized within themselves the hope that God had implanted in them, and with hope cried their cries for freedom and justice."[27]

"As we were" plants Mandela firmly in the tradition of centuries of struggle, in the midst of a people who knew, in the most tragic circumstances, the one thing that stood between

27. See Boesak, *The Tenderness of Conscience*, p. 240.

Dare We Speak of Hope?

them and despair: that heaven has not deserted us. He spoke from the heart of a people who understood that struggle was never easy; that the road to freedom is always via the cross; that we struggle for justice because we need to bestow on Africa and the world the greatest of all gifts – a human face.[28]

"As we were" reminds us that the Freedom Charter, whose spirit guides our constitution, was born of the pain of suffering as well as of the joy of faith: "South Africa belongs to all who live in it, black and white." Those were not words of empty optimism or shallow bravado. Spoken in 1955, in the face of a regime determined to subdue, subject, and suppress black people, they were words of defiant hope in the midst of death, words denying hatred and vengeance, hopelessness and despair, any place in our country or in our hearts.

"As we were" recalls the millions who believed that our struggle for justice should not just be for ourselves but a "blessing for humankind," as Robert Sobukwe believed.[29] Those who stood up in the Defiance campaigns of the 1950s; those who died in the Sharpeville Massacre in 1960, and in the streets of deadly confrontation since then; Steve Biko and the bright young minds who helped shape our philosophy of black consciousness in the 1970s and helped us to stand tall and proud; the brave youth of Soweto who marched in 1976, inspiring a whole new generation across the country, forever changing the shape of the struggle; the unstoppable, multiracial masses who formed the United Democratic Front and stormed the gates of apartheid's citadels in the 1980s; the brave mine workers of today who have taken on the brutality of a government that forgot

28. Steve Biko, *I Write What I Like* (Johannesburg: Ravan Press, 1996), p. 98.

29. See Tom Karis and Gwendolyn Carter, *From Protest to Challenge*, vol. 2 (Stanford: Stanford University Press, 1973,), p. 332.

the price of freedom even as it claims to be freedom's vessel; and the millions who simply refused to give up and who saw Satan fall like lightning from heaven.

With the words "as we were," Mandela placed himself and the people of South Africa in the midst of the world community, wherever there is injustice, pain, and struggle, and wherever people still seek Hope and find her in their stride toward freedom — vivid, real, audacious, unstoppable.

So is this the answer to the question of how we protect our politicians against the corruption of the empire once they sit in the seat of power, whereby they only seem to understand their call to administer justice once they have left office, as we have seen over and over again? Perhaps it is possible, if we insist that when we trust them with our votes and our lives, and we vest them with our power, that they in turn trust us with helping them keep their promises and their hopes, their vision, and their legitimacy. If President Obama can return to the people and call on them for help in his struggle against Republicans to stop short of a "fiscal cliff" (which includes a fairer tax system), why doesn't he call on them for help on the greater, more fundamental issues of ending the wars, eradicating poverty, and creating systemic justice? The nature of our politics might change if the first instincts of our politicians who claim to believe in the politics of hope and justice — Mandela's "cadre of leadership" — would be to trust and respond to the people who vested them with their power instead of seeking the false safety of the empire they think they need to keep them in power. Would that not be a different kind of participatory democracy? It is "we, the people" — we, the resilient, hopeful people — who must keep them true to what they claim to believe, and it is only the people who can give meaning to the phrase "we are in this together."

If we continue in this hope, we will also better understand

former South African president Thabo Mbeki's wise words when he spoke of the difficulties facing Africa today: "The challenge we face cannot reside merely in the recognition and acknowledgment of what is wrong. Principally it consists in answering the question correctly: What must be done to ensure that the right thing is done?"[30]

So, instead of mindlessly deifying Mandela as the world has so consistently done, thereby making his acts of magnanimity and justice unattainable and his words of hope meaningless for "ordinary" human beings, the world might simply try to learn from the life of this man who referred to himself as "ancient as the hills of Qunu": that old hatreds do not pass of their own volition; they have to be challenged and overcome by the power of love and the resilience of reconciliation. That the lines of tribe will not dissolve on their own; they have to be overcome by our belief in and our work toward our common humanity. That that common humanity, in turn, will only reveal itself in the undoing of injustice and the doing of justice, the embrace of our diversity in dignity and respect, and our common concern for the well-being of the earth. That a new era of peace will not be ushered in on the wings of historical inevitabilities, but only through the hard and persistent work toward the ending of war, aggression, terror, and the idolatrous worship of violence as the solution to all our problems. And it is work we shall do together, and not give up "until justice and peace embrace."

With President Obama now in his second term of office, and our hope irresistibly springing up again, we should take care to remind him of the power and promise of his own words from those days when hopeful politics was held up as a blessing, not a curse, a gateway and not a dead-end street. We need

30. Thabo Mbeki, *Africa: The Time Has Come* (Cape Town: Tafelberg, 1998), p. 206.

Only If We Speak of Dreaming   173

to prophetically hold him accountable, letting him know that, once again, "our moment is now." In so doing, we will encourage him infinitely more than any mindless sycophancy ever can. "Hope is not blind optimism. It is not ignoring the enormity of the task before us or the roadblocks that stand in our path. . . . That is the power of hope – to imagine and then to work for what seemed impossible before. . . ."[31]

Perhaps we also do well to remember that in all this work we should not look for approval from the powerful, or even for admiration from the powerless, but should humbly accept Christian theologian Tony Campolo's wise counsel to President Obama, and thus to every person who sits in the seats of power, that "the only applause [we] should seek is that which comes from nail-pierced hands."[32]

31. Barack Obama, "Our Moment Is Now," remarks made in Des Moines, IA, Dec. 27, 2007, quoted in Mitzi J. Smith, "The Hopeology of Barack Obama: Biblical Reflections and Personal Musings," in McMickle, *The Audacity of Faith*, p. 15.

32. See Tony Campolo, "Hope Has Its Reasons," in McMickle, *The Audacity of Faith*, p. 98.

Dare We Speak of Hope?

The Hope Conundrum

A Meditation

*Here is my servant, whom I uphold, my chosen, in whom
my soul delights; I have put my spirit upon him; he will
bring forth justice to the nations. He will not cry or lift up
his voice in the street; a bruised reed he will not break, and
a dimly burning wick he will not quench; he will faithfully
bring forth justice. He will not grow faint or be crushed
until he has established justice in the earth; and the coastlands wait for his teaching.*

Isaiah 42:1-4

And in his name the Gentiles will hope.

Matthew 12:21

Throughout this book I have talked about hope, faith, and politics — the tensions, the challenges, the possibilities. We have
found that we in South Africa are now not as emphatically eu-
phoric about our politics as we once were. We hope, sometimes
against hope, that the next term will bring the fulfillment of

hopes that were disappointed in the preceding term, or that South Africa and the world will somehow find and raise those visionaries who will become Mandela's "cadre of leaders," those who will understand and honor the demands of justice for God's people. We are hopeful, but not at all certain, that this will happen: "Even if it takes another hundred years," write the churches in an almost defiant tone in the letter I quoted in the introduction, "we are determined to begin the journey forthwith."

Mandela's "long road to freedom," we now understand better than in the giddy days of 1994, is far from ended. In fact, it has not yet turned its first bend. We have, it seems, a hope conundrum, that is, a "paradoxical, insoluble problem," according to the dictionary, "a dilemma." Politics is a vortex of expectations, disillusionments, and bewilderments, but we cannot step away from it or from our commitment to make it work for justice. Hope holds us captive; we cannot give her up, let go of her hand, lest we become utterly lost. Yet we now know that where she is to be found is not in the places of comfort and safety, and certainly not unreservedly in the politics that we have invested with so much hope and faith.

Time and time again, it seems, we have to learn the lesson that while our hope has to shape our politics, the center of our hope never lies in politics or politicians. Christians have to look elsewhere if we are to find a hope that is durable, life-affirming, and life-giving. If we are to challenge and change the world, which is our calling and the purpose of our life, and if we are to run this race and persevere, we must, as the book of Hebrews teaches us, keep "looking to Jesus the pioneer and perfecter of our faith" (Heb. 12:2 [RSV]). Both Isaiah and Matthew tell us why.

Isaiah, speaking from within the context of the Babylonian/Persian empires, and Matthew, speaking within the context of the Roman empire, were both seeking to encourage and strengthen their oppressed and exploited communities. Isaiah points to the servant of Yahweh, and Matthew identifies him as Jesus of Nazareth. Both declare God's purpose with this servant: to bring justice in the earth, so that the world may have hope and joy. In other words, to say "Jesus" is to say "justice," and to say "justice" is to say "hope."

When we understand this, we understand how blasphemous it is to carve the name "Jesus" into the sides of a slavetrader boat, how blasphemous it is to create a policy as hellish and destructive as apartheid and then invoke the name of Jesus over it. When we grasp this, it is also clear how blasphemous it is to make war, to maim and kill and destroy, and then to justify it all in the name of Jesus. How blasphemous it is to baptize our racism, bigotry, greed, patriarchy, sexism, homophobia, and all our fears of and resistance to otherness in the name of Jesus and call it "Christian." How blasphemous it is to diminish others and thus deny the image of God in them, to marginalize them or exclude them altogether, and to call that "Christian."

The servant of Yahweh whom Isaiah talks about and the Jesus whom Matthew holds up as the hope of the Gentiles – he is the one who brings justice in the earth. Three times in four verses Isaiah repeats it in tones of rising emphasis:

- he will bring forth justice;
- he will *faithfully* bring forth justice;
- he will *establish* justice.

He will – and Isaiah is emphatic so that we do not miss this crucial point – establish justice *in the earth*. Not just in Jerusalem or in Judea, and not for Israel only. *In the earth*. It is an enduring commitment that he will faithfully execute, not just talk about, debate, think on, ponder, and weigh its acceptability in the eyes of those who seek to control the world as he constantly looks over his shoulder. He *will* establish justice. That is why Matthew takes the liberty of changing Isaiah's "the coastlands await his teaching" to "in his name will the Gentiles hope." Matthew wants no misunderstanding: his use of "Gentiles" denotes all the world. And it is not just about waiting, he seems to say; it is about *hoping*. There is an unmistakable urgency in that word. It strains toward active engagement with the future. It is not that the Gentiles are patiently waiting; they are reaching forward to grasp it, opening themselves to receive it, ready to embrace it. There is a holy eagerness in Matthew's words.

Up front is the guarantee and foundation of our faith and hope in him. He is Yahweh's chosen, the one Yahweh will "uphold," the one in whom Yahweh's soul "delights": "I have put my spirit upon him." His calling is not merely the undoing of injustice and the doing of justice; he will bring justice to *victory*. This is not a mere declaration of intent; it is God's commitment until the task is fulfilled.

In this work – in order to establish justice and bring it to victory – there are, Isaiah is at pains to make clear, three things this servant will not do. First, he will not raise his voice in the streets; second, he will not break a bruised reed; and third, he will not quench the smoldering wick. But what do these things mean? Let's ponder them one by one, for this is how Isaiah distinguishes the servant of Yahweh from the pretenders, those who claim to do justice but in reality serve only the interests of the empire and the powerful within the empire, those who call exploitation "justice," who call oppression "containment," and who call violent destruction "peace."

"He will not cry or lift up his voice in the street." This does not mean that he will not ever speak of justice or proclaim the reign of God as diametrically opposed to the caesar's empire. His voice, though, will be entirely different from the voices emanating from the empire: it will be a countervoice. The voices the people hear in the streets, the voices reverberating from the places of power and fear, are the voices of Rome, its heralds shouting "Bow down!" and "Make way!" before the horses and the chariots carrying the ruling elites, scattering the people to the side of the road. They are the voices speaking for the caesar and the pharaoh, pronouncing unjust laws, demanding submission to the occupying power, announcing punishment and death. They are the voices of its governors and rulers, its tax collectors and commanders and soldiers, the voices of endless aggression, intimidation, scorn, and violent oppression.

The voices that the people hear are the voices of those who deem it their right to pray loudly in the synagogues and on street corners, virtually shouting their superior holiness to that of the common folk (Matt. 6:5). They are the voices of the ruling elites in Jerusalem: the priests who harangue the poor for their tithes and taxes, exploiting the people's love of God; the voices of the scribes and lawyers who pontificate about the Torah, threatening the people with their fear of God. Those voices who demand "tithes of mint, dill and cumin, but neglect the weightier matters of the law — justice, mercy, and faith." These are voices of oppression, humiliation, disdain, and condemnation. They are voices of death. Amid these voices, the servant is silent, but hers is not the silence that acquiesces. It is the silence that exposes and shames.

"He will not break the bruised reed." That is, the servant will not consider anyone worthless, or not worth the effort, or useless trash (such as broken reeds are), or as disposable, dispensable, and forgettable. Nor will he regard God's children as the byproduct of intentional violence and call them "collateral damage," as if their lives did not matter because they are poor, or defenseless, or different. It means that the servant will not exploit people's powerlessness or manipulate their weaknesses, or feed on their fears, or gloat over their woundability, or prey on their vulnerability and their hurts for political gain, or use the bewilderment he causes to create even more confusion, because he brings justice to victory and he is the hope of the nations.

"He will not quench a smoldering wick." Being who he is, the servant of Yahweh will not smother someone's hopes no matter how fragile, or reduce them to helpless hopelessness. He will not rob them of their dignity, steal their dreams, or mock their ideals for the sake of political expediency, ideological gain, or self-aggrandizement, for he brings justice to victory and is the hope of the nations. Those who are battered and broken, excluded and discarded, broken down and looked down upon, despised and stigmatized — he will not send them away bleeding, untended, burdened, and empty-handed.

When he has done all that, he will do one more thing. For their sake, Isaiah says, he will not grow faint or weary, nor will he allow himself to be crushed — *until he has brought justice in the earth*. This God is in it for the duration.

Oh, they will *try* to crush him. Of course they will; the response to the bringer of hope and the dreamer of dreams is always murderous. Isaiah knows that the servant of Yahweh will become the suffering servant. They will deny him, resist him, vilify him, demonize him, falsely accuse him, reject him; but he will not grow weary. He will not give up, will not get tired, will not look for an easier way. He will stand with us and stand up for us, fight for us, face hostility, endure suffering, die on the cross. But he will rise again and will refuse to be crushed until he has established justice in the earth. In his name will the Gentiles hope.

Now, from Isaiah 42:6 onward, God turns around and looks at the people. "I am the LORD, I have called you in righteousness, I have taken you by the hand and kept you. . . ." Right through this struggle, God says, my servant has been with you, committed not to give up until justice is brought to victory. But you have survived and were able to join me in that struggle because it is I who have called you to righteousness. On your own, you would have failed, looked for ways out, could not have stayed the course; but I have taken you by the hand and kept you. The imagery here is intensely moving and utterly stunning in its intimacy.

Here Yahweh speaks of the glory that struggle holds, though it is not yet seen: "I have given you as a covenant to the people, a light to the nations." But that gift of the covenant, of being a "light to the nations," is not for self-glorification. It is not a psychological crutch that must help us through the moments of darkness as we are exposed to the shocking realities our heresies create. Nor is it a blanket, preemptive justification for our arrogance, by which we claim for ourselves a "manifest destiny," an exceptionalism Jesus himself has shunned. Chosenness — being a light to the nations — has a greater purpose: "to open the eyes that are blind, to bring out the prisoners from the dungeon, from the prison those who sit in darkness." The vessels of the covenant are called to deeds of liberation and justice, thereby bringing hope to "those who sit in darkness."

And it is only when we do this, when we join the servant of Yahweh in the struggle to establish justice in the earth, that the silence is broken. It is a sublime turn in the passage. All along, the servant of Yahweh is the silent one, not raising her voice, not being heard in the streets. Now, though, when God's people join God in the struggle to bring justice to victory and hope to the nations, there is joyful noise everywhere. There is a new song to the Lord and praise "from the ends of the earth." The sea "and all that fills it" roars, and the nations of the earth join in praise. The deserts and their towns "lift up their voice."

Then, like a photographer with a trained eye, Isaiah zooms

in: "The villages of Kedar, the inhabitants of Sela" — they all "sing for joy." It is a phrase the prophet cannot seem to get enough of. "Let them shout from the tops of the mountains!" Isaiah himself seems to be shouting now. "Let them give glory to the LORD, and declare his praise in the coastlands!" All this joy is contagious. The joyful noise reverberates around in the earth and resounds to the heavens, and it is not the angels who sing for the joy that is on earth, it is Yahweh who now joins the celebrations and "cries out, he shouts aloud, he shows himself mighty against his foes."

One feels like stopping for a moment, to catch one's breath, and then ask the question that all this evokes: Why?

All because justice is being brought to victory. Hope and her daughters are vindicated. There is no conundrum, no insoluble dilemma. Not anymore. Now it is no longer a lone woman playing the one string on her broken harp, torn and bruised, and she herself desolate amid the devastation of the world. Now there are multitudes — God's whole world — singing praises. We are *all* God's covenant, God's light to each other. Godself is singing and dancing with us in delighted abandon. Now we shall no longer sing *senzenina* — the time of our mourning is over. We do not even have to sing *thuma mina* — the One who sent us is with us. Now we sing *ukanamandla uSatani*, for it *is* broken; the power of Satan, it is broken! Hallelujah!

Bibliography

Books

Alexander, Michelle. *The New Jim Crow: Mass Incarceration in the Age of Colorblindness.* New York: New Press, 2010.

Ali, Tariq. *The Obama Syndrome: Surrender at Home, War Abroad.* London and New York: Verso, 2010.

Amjad-Ali, Charles. *Islamophobia or Restorative Justice: Tearing the Veil of Ignorance.* Johannesburg: Ditshwanelo Car'as, 2006.

Asmal, Kader, Louise Asmal, and Ronald Suresh Roberts. *Reconciliation Through Truth: A Reckoning of Apartheid's Criminal Governance.* Cape Town: David Philip, 1999.

Bacevich, Andrew J. *The New American Militarism: How Americans Are Seduced by War.* New York: Oxford University Press, 2005.

Bell, Derrick. *Faces at the Bottom of the Well: The Permanence of Racism.* New York: Basic Books, 1992.

Biko, Steve. *I Write What I Like: A Selection of His Writings.* Johannesburg: Ravan Press, 2005.

Boesak, Allan. *Die Vlug van Gods Verbeelding: Bybelverhale van die Onderkant (The Flight of God's Imagination: Biblical Stories from the Underside).* Stellenbosch: Sun Press, 2005.

————. *Farewell to Innocence: A Socio-Ethical Study on Black Theology and Black Power.* Maryknoll, NY: Orbis, 1977.

————. *Running with Horses: Reflections of an Accidental Politician.* Cape Town: JoHo! Publications, 2009.

————. *The Tenderness of Conscience: African Renaissance and the Spirituality of Politics.* Stellenbosch: Sun Press, 2005.

————. *Walking on Thorns: The Call to Christian Obedience.* Geneva: WCC, 1984; Grand Rapids: Eerdmans, 1984.

Boesak, Allan, and Curtiss Paul DeYoung. *Radical Reconciliation: Beyond Political Pietism and Christian Quietism.* Maryknoll, NY: Orbis, 2012.

Boesak, Allan, Johann Weusmann, and Charles Amjad-Ali, eds. *Dreaming a Different World: Globalisation and Justice for Humanity and the Earth; The Challenge of the Accra Confession for the Churches.* Stellenbosch: The Globalisation Project, 2010.

Boezak, Willa. *So Glo Ons! Die Khoe-San van Suid-Afrika.* Kimberley: Northern Cape Province Ministry for Environmental Affairs and Tourism, 2007.

Bonhoeffer, Dietrich. *Barcelona, Berlin, New York: 1928-1931.* Clifford J. Green, editor. Dietrich Bonhoeffer Works, vol. 10. Minneapolis: Fortress, 2008.

————. *Berlin: 1932-1933.* Larry L. Rasmussen and Isabel Best, editors. Dietrich Bonhoeffer Works, vol. 12. Minneapolis: Fortress, 2009.

————. *London, 1933-1935.* Keith W. Clements, editor. Dietrich Bonhoeffer Works, vol. 13. Minneapolis: Fortress, 2007.

————. *Theological Education at Finkenwalde: 1935-1937.* H. Gaylon Barker and Mark Brocker, editors. Dietrich Bonhoeffer Works, vol. 14. Minneapolis: Fortress, 2013.

Bonino, José Miguez. *Toward a Christian Political Ethics.* Philadelphia: Fortress, 1983.

Boyd, Gregory A. *The Myth of a Christian Nation: How the Quest for Political Power Is Destroying the Church.* Grand Rapids: Zondervan, 2005.

Brown, Robert McAfee. *Spirituality and Liberation: Overcoming the Great Fallacy.* Philadelphia: Westminster, 1988.

Brueggemann, Walter. *First and Second Samuel.* Interpretation, A Bible Commentary for Teaching and Preaching. James Luther Mays, Patrick D. Miller, and Paul J. Achtemeier, general editors. Louisville: John Knox, 1990.

————. *Genesis.* Interpretation, A Bible Commentary for Preaching and Teaching. James Luther Mays, general editor. Atlanta: John Knox, 1982.

————. *The Prophetic Imagination.* Minneapolis: Fortress, 2001.

Calvin, John. *Commentaries on the Twelve Minor Prophets,* vol. 4: *Habakkuk, Zephaniah, Haggai.* Grand Rapids: Eerdmans, 1950.

Chomski, Noam. *Year 501: The Conquest Continues.* Boston: South End Press, 1993.

Claassens, Juliana M. *Mother, Mourner and Midwife: Reimagining God's Delivering Presence in the Old Testament.* Louisville: Westminster John Knox, 2012.

Claassens, Juliana, and Stella Viljoen, eds. *Sacred Selves: Essays on Gender, Religion, and Popular Culture.* Cape Town: Griffel, 2012.

Cone, James H. *The Cross and the Lynching Tree.* Maryknoll, NY: Orbis, 2012.

————. *God of the Oppressed.* Revised edition. Maryknoll, NY: Orbis, 1997.

Davidson, Robert. *Genesis 12–50.* The Cambridge Bible Commentary on the New English Bible. Cambridge: Cambridge University Press, 1979.

Dyson, Michael Eric. *Debating Race with Michael Eric Dyson.* New York: Basic Civitas Books, 2007.

Falk, Richard. *The Great Terror War.* New York: Olive Branch Press, 2003.

Ferguson, John. *War and Peace in the World's Religions.* New York: Oxford University Press, 1978.

Griffin, David Ray, John B. Cobb, Richard A. Falk, and Catherine

Keller. *The American Empire and the Commonwealth of God: A Political, Economic, Religious Statement.* Louisville: Westminster John Knox, 2006.

Hahn, Theophilus. *Tsuni//Goam: The Supreme Being of the Khoi-Khoi.* London: Juta, 1881.

Hamilton, Victor P. *The Book of Genesis, Chapters 18–50.* New International Commentary on the Old Testament. Grand Rapids: Eerdmans, 1995.

Havel, Vaclav. *Summer Meditations.* Translated by Paul Wilson. New York: Alfred A. Knopf, 1992.

Hawken, Paul. *Blessed Unrest: How the Largest Social Movement in History Is Restoring Grace, Justice and Beauty to the World.* New York: Penguin, 2007.

Hendricks, Obery M., Jr. *The Politics of Jesus: Rediscovering the True Revolutionary Nature of Jesus' Teachings and How They Have Been Corrupted.* New York: Doubleday, 2006.

Herbert, T. Walter. *Faith-Based War: From 9/11 to Catastrophic Success in Iraq.* London and Oakville: Equinox Press, 2009.

Holmes, Arthur F., ed. *War and Christian Ethics.* Grand Rapids: Baker Book House, 1975.

Hopkins, Dwight N. *Down, Up, and Over: Slave Religion and Black Theology.* Minneapolis: Fortress, 2000.

Ilibagiza, Immaculée. *Left to Tell: Discovering God Amidst the Rwandan Holocaust.* Carlsbad, CA: Hay House, 2006.

Jensen, Robert. *Citizens of the Empire: The Struggle to Claim Our Humanity.* San Francisco: City Lights Books, 2004.

Kaplan, Lawrence F., and William Kristol. *The War Over Iraq: Saddam's Tyranny and America's Mission.* San Francisco: Encounter Books, 2003.

Karis, Tom, and Gwendolyn Carter. *From Protest to Challenge.* Vol. 2. Stanford: Stanford University Press, 1973.

Keller, Catherine. *God and Power: Counter-Apocalyptic Journeys.* Minneapolis: Fortress, 2005.

Kimball, Charles. *When Religion Becomes Evil*. San Francisco: Harper-SanFrancisco, 2002.

L'Ange, Gerard. *The White Africans: From Colonisation to Liberation*. Johannesburg and Cape Town: Jonathan Ball Publishers, 2005.

Linebaugh, Peter, and Marcus Rediker. *The Many-Headed Hydra: Sailors, Slaves and Commoners, and the Hidden History of the Revolutionary Atlantic*. Boston: Beacon, 2000.

Longacre, Robert E. *Joseph: A Story of Divine Providence*. Winona Lake, IN: Eisenbrauns, 1989.

Lowenthal, Eric I. *The Joseph Narrative in Genesis: An Interpretation*. New York: KTAV Publishing House, 1973.

Luthuli, Albert. *Let My People Go!* Cape Town: Tafelberg, 2006.

Macy, Joanna, and Molly Young Brown. *Coming Back to Life: Practices to Reconnect Our Lives, Our World*. Gabriola Island, Canada: New Society Publishers, 1998.

Magona, Sindiwe. *Mother to Mother*. Cape Town: David Philip, 1998.

Mahajan, Rahul. *The New Crusade: America's War on Terrorism*. New York: Monthly Review Press, 2002.

Mamdani, Mahmood. *Good Muslim, Bad Muslim: America, the Cold War and the Roots of Terror*. 4th edition. Johannesburg: Jacana Media, 2007.

Marsh, Charles. *Wayward Christian Soldiers: Freeing the Gospel from Political Captivity*. New York: Oxford University Press, 2007.

Mbeki, Thabo. *Africa: The Time Has Come*. Cape Town: Tafelberg, and Johannesburg: Mafube, 1998.

Ministry of Reconciliation. *From Beloved Community to Communities of Hope: A Small-Group Study Guide to Engaging Reconciliation*. Indianapolis: Christian Church (Disciples of Christ), 2009.

Mofokeng, Tokatso. *The Crucified Among the Cross-bearers: Towards a Black Christology*. Kampen: Kok, 1983.

Mosoeta, Sarah. *Eating from One Pot*. Johannesburg: Wits University Press, 2011.

Obama, Barack. *The Audacity of Hope: Thoughts on Reclaiming the American Dream.* London: Canongate Publishers, 2006.

Palmer, Parker J. *Healing the Heart of Democracy: The Courage to Create a Politics Worthy of the Human Spirit.* San Francisco: Jossey-Bass, 2011.

Pauw, Jacques. *Dances with Devils: A Journalist's Search for Truth.* Cape Town: Zebra Press, 2006.

Roop, Eugene F. *Genesis.* Believer's Church Bible Commentary. Scottdale, PA: Herald Press, 1987.

Rothenberg, Paula S. *Race, Class and Gender in the United States.* 8th edition. New York: Worth Publications, 2010.

Sacks, Jonathan. *The Dignity of Difference: How to Avoid the Clash of Civilizations.* New York and London: Continuum, 2006.

Schlingensiepen, Ferdinand. *Dietrich Bonhoeffer 1906-1945: Martyr, Thinker, Man of Resistance.* London: T&T Clark International, 2010.

Stephanson, Ander. *Manifest Destiny: American Expansion and the Empire of Right.* New York: Hill and Wang, 1995.

Tennyson, Alfred Lord. *Poems.* Edited by Hallam Lord Tennyson. London: Macmillan, 1908.

Ter Schegget, G. *De Andere Mogelijkheid.* Baarn, The Netherlands: Ten Have, 1973.

Terreblanche, Sampie. *Lost in Transformation: South Africa's Search for a New Future Since 1986.* Johannesburg: KMM Review Publishing, 2012.

Thomas, Frank A. *The American Dream 2.0: A Christian Way Out of the Great Recession.* Nashville: Abingdon, 2012.

Townes, Emilie, ed. *A Troubling in My Soul: Womanist Perspectives on Evil and Suffering.* Maryknoll, NY: Orbis, 1993.

Van Aarde, Andries. *Fatherless in Galilee: Jesus as Child of God.* Harrisburg, PA: Trinity Press International, 2001.

Van Selms, A. *Genesis Deel II: De Prediking van het Oude Testament.* Nijkerk, Netherlands: Uitgeverij Callenbach NV, 1976.

Villa-Vicencio, Charles. *Walk with Us and Listen: Political Reconciliation in Africa*. Cape Town: UCT Press, 2010.

Wallis, Jim, and Joyce Hollyday, eds. *Crucible of Fire: The Church Confronts Apartheid*. Maryknoll, NY: Orbis, 1987.

Westermann, Claus. *Genesis 37-50: A Commentary*. London: SPCK, 1986.

Wilmore, Gayraud S. *Black Religion and Black Radicalism: An Interpretation of the Religious History of African Americans*. Maryknoll, NY: Orbis, 1973.

Wink, Walter. *The Powers That Be: Theology for a New Millennium*. New York: Galilee Doubleday, 2001.

Wright, Jeremiah. *What Makes You So Strong? Sermons of Joy and Strength*. Edited by Jini M. Kilgore. Valley Forge, PA: Judson Press, 1993.

Articles

Ali, Tariq. "From Shoes to Soft Drinks to Underpants." *The Economist*, December 30, 2010.

Alves, Rubem. "Christian Realism: Ideology of the Establishment." *Christianity and Crisis*, September 17, 1973.

Boesak, Allan. "To Stand Where God Stands." *Studia Historiae Ecclesiasticae* 34, no. 1 (July 2008): 143-72.

Braxton, Brad R. "Hope in 3-D." In *The Audacity of Faith: Christian Leaders Reflect on the Election of Barack Obama*, edited by Marvin A. McMickle. Valley Forge, PA: Judson Press, 2009.

Breck, John. "Justifiable War: Lesser Good or Lesser Evil?" *St. Vladimir's Theological Quarterly* 47, no. 1 (2003).

Buthelezi, Manas. "Violence and the Cross in South Africa." *Journal of Theology for Southern Africa* (December 1979).

Campolo, Tony. "Hope Has Its Reasons." In *The Audacity of Faith: Christian Leaders Reflect on the Election of Barack Obama*, edited by Marvin A. McMickle. Valley Forge, PA: Judson Press, 2009.

Clough, David, and Brian Stiltner. "On the Importance of Drawn Swords: Christian Thinking about Preemptive War – and Its Modern Outworking." *Journal of the Society of Christian Ethics* 27, no. 2 (2007).

Elverton Dixon, Valerie. "Barack Obama and the American Civil Religion." In *The Audacity of Faith: Christian Leaders Reflect on the Election of Barack Obama*, edited by Marvin A. McMickle. Valley Forge, PA: Judson Press, 2009.

Graham, Bob. "I just pulled the trigger." In *Evening Standard* (UK), June 19, 2003: http://www.eswheels.co.uk/news/articles/5402104

Keller, Catherine. "Omnipotence and Preemption." In *The American Empire and the Commonwealth of God: A Political, Economic, Religious Statement*, edited by David Ray Griffin, John B. Cobb Jr., Richard A. Falk, and Catherine Keller. Louisville: Westminster John Knox, 2006.

King, Martin Luther, Jr. "A Time to Break the Silence." In *A Testament of Hope: The Essential Writings of Martin Luther King, Jr.* Edited by James M. Washington. San Francisco: Harper and Row, 1986.

———. "Shattered Dreams." In *Strength to Love*. Philadelphia: Fortress Press, 1963.

Murray, Christopher J., Sandeep Kulkarni, and Majid Ezzati. "Eight Americas: New Perspectives on U.S. Health Disparities." *American Journal of Preventive Medicine* 29, no. 5, Suppl. 1 (2005).

Myers, William H. "A Hope That Does Not Disappoint." In *The Audacity of Faith: Christian Leaders Reflect on the Election of Barack Obama*, edited by Marvin A. McMickle. Valley Forge: Judson Press, 2009.

Ntsikana, John. "The Shade of a Fabulous Ghost." In *ES'KIA, Education, African Humanities and Culture, Social Consciousness, Literary Appreciation*, edited by Es'kia Mphahlele. Johannesburg: Kwela Books, 2002.

Omar, Irfan A. "Islam." In *The Hope of Liberation in World Religions*, edited by Miguel A. De La Torre. Waco: Baylor University Press, 2008.

Smith, J. Alfred. "God's Invisible Hand." In *The Audacity of Faith: Christian Leaders Reflect on the Election of Barack Obama*, edited by Marvin A. McMickle. Valley Forge, PA: Judson Press, 2009.

Smith, Robin L. "Dreaming Like a Fool." In *The Audacity of Faith: Christian Leaders Reflect on the Election of Barack Obama*, edited by Marvin A. McMickle. Valley Forge: Judson Press, 2009.

Sottile, J. P. "Boldly going where only drones have gone before." Reader Supported News: http://www.readersupportednews.org.opinion2/282-98/7968 (accessed Sept. 19, 2011).

Stewart, Gina M. "Almost But Not Quite." In *The Audacity of Faith: Christian Leaders Reflect on the Election of Barack Obama*, edited by Marvin A. McMickle. Valley Forge, PA: Judson Press, 2009.

Stiglitz, Joseph. "The 1 Percent's Problem." *Vanity Fair*, June 2, 2012: readersupportednews.org/opinion2/279-82/11727-focus-the-1-per-cents-problem (accessed June 2, 2012).

"US Has Second-Highest Rate of Childhood Poverty in Developed World, Only Romania Is Worse." *International Business Times*: http://www.ibtimes.com/us-has-second-highest-rate-childhood -poverty-developed-world (accessed Nov. 20, 2012).

Warnock, Raphael. "Dreams from Our Fathers." In *The Audacity of Faith: Christian Leaders Reflect on the Election of Barack Obama*, edited by Marvin A. McMickle. Valley Forge, PA: Judson Press, 2009.

Webster, Alexander F. C. "Justifiable War as a 'Lesser Good' in Eastern Orthodox Moral Tradition." *St. Vladimir's Theological Quarterly* 37, no. 1 (2003).

Willimon, William H. "Preacher-Prophet Obama." In *The Audacity of Faith: Christian Leaders Reflect on the Election of Barack Obama*, edited by Marvin A. McMickle. Valley Forge, PA: Judson Press, 2009.

Woodill, Joseph. "Justifiable War: Response #1." *St. Vladimir's Theological Quarterly* 47, no. 1 (2003).

Other

"Accra Confession": *That All May Have Life in Fullness: World Alliance of Reformed Churches' 24th General Council Proceedings.* Geneva: World Alliance of Reformed Churches, 2005.

"The Belhar Confession." *World Alliance of Reformed Churches, Semper Reformanda:* www.wcrc.ch/belhar-confession/.

"The church speaks . . . for such a time as this," open letter to the African National Congress from the SACC, TEASA, African Enterprise, and Kairos SA, issued December 2, 2012.

The Freedom Charter: http://www.anc.org.za/show.php?id=72

Kairos SA. *Call to Action: U.S. Response to Kairos Palestine Document,* 2012.

Kairos SA. *The Kairos Document.* South Africa, 1985.

Kairos SA. *Kairos Palestine: A Moment of Truth; A Word of Faith, Hope and Love from the Heart of Palestinian Suffering,* 2009.

"National Defense Authorization Act for Fiscal Year 2012": http://en.wikipedia.org.wiki/National_Defense_Authorization_Act_for_Fiscal_Year_2012; http://en.wikipedia.org/wiki/Military_budget_of_the_United_States (accessed Nov. 20, 2012).

The Natives Land Act, 27 of 1913.

Obama, Barack. Acceptance Speech for the Nobel Peace Prize: http://www.msnbc.msn.com/od/34360743/ns/politics-white-house/t/full-text-obama's-nobel-peace-prize-speech (accessed December 5, 2012).

South Africa's Women's March (Women's Day): http://encyclopedia2.the_freedictionary.com/South+Africa+women%27s+Day

Testimony in the Treason Trial: http://www.anc.org.za/ancdocs/history/lutuli/lutulii8.html#six8 (accessed April 6, 2012).

UNICEF: http://www.unicef.org

United Nations. *United Nations Development Report.* New York: United Nations, 1997.

Index

as female/feminine, 19; hope known in encounter with suffering and struggle, 70; and Hope's girl children, Anger and Courage, 43, 44-50, 62, 151; and just-war tradition, 112, 116

Bacevich, Andrew J., 111-12
Barker, H. Gaylon, 15n
Barrett, Frank J., 108n
Belhar Confession of the Uniting Reformed Church in Southern Africa, 49-50
Bell, Derrick, 42n
Best, Isabel, 17n
Biko, Steve, 25, 118, 171
Bin Laden, Osama, 96-99, 112
Boer rebellions, 69
Boezak, Willa, 35n, 36, 37n
Bonhoeffer, Dietrich, 14-18, 20; chastisement of "pagans," 86-87; decision to be faithful to the earth (for the sake of the things above), 27-28; decision to enter the politics of resistance, 16-18; decision to "stand up without compromise," 14-18; finding the place where Christ stands, 16, 80-81; hope and struggle, 80-81, 85-87; resistance against Hitler/Nazism, 14-18, 80-81; standing with God in God's grieving, 85-87
Bonino, José Miguez, 21
Boyd, Gregory A., 106n
Braxton, Brad R., 4n, 136n
Breck, John, 112-13, 114
Brocker, Mark, 15n
Brown, Molly Young, 139n
Brown, Robert McAfee, 43n
Brueggemann, Walter, 47n, 59, 137-38, 158, 165-66, 168
Bush, George W./Bush administration, 11, 95, 97, 102-3, 111, 138n

Buthelezi, Manas, 142

Calvin, John, 32-33, 82-83, 94, 112
Campolo, Tony, 136n, 174
Carson, Rachel, 53-54
Carter, Gwendolyn, 171n
Chechnya, 105
Children: child-soldiers and children of war, 88; discontent and our obligations as God's children, 50-60, 65-66; Hope's girl children, 43, 44-50, 62, 151; the marginalized children of ancient Israel, 46-47; poverty and economic inequality, 10, 61; targeted sanctions and Iraqi deaths, 104, 138n; trafficked, 88. *See also* Children of Hope
Children of Hope, 43-66, 89; Accra Confession, 51-60; Augustine and Hope's daughters, Anger and Courage, 43, 44-50, 62, 151; and the Belhar Confession, 49-50; and challenge to patriarchy, 48-49; and demands for justice, 44-45; and the hope of discontent, 50-60, 65-66; the marginalized children of ancient Israel, 46-47; personalization of hope, 44; seeing the world through the eyes of the poor and suffering, 62-65
Chisholm, Shirley, 136n
Chomsky, Noam, 101n
Claassens, Juliana M., 39-40, 108n
Clements, Keith W., 14n
Clinton, Bill, 138n
Clough, David, 111n
Cobb, John B., Jr., 39n, 102n
Cold War, 91, 117
Cole, Darryl, 110
Colonial wars, 91-93
Cone, James H., 2, 141n
Congo, Democratic Republic of, 91

Conviction, faith, and hope, 33
Council for World Mission (CWM)
Assembly's "statement of discontent," 50-51, 127-28
Couper, Scott, 76n
Courage. *See* Children of Hope
Cowan, Collin, 50
Creation: crisis of, 51; and the Khoi people's wounded God, 34-38. *See also* Ecological destruction
Criminal justice system, U.S., 10-11
Cynicism: and the ANC, 1-2, 6-10; politics of, 1-14; resisting, 26-27. *See also* Politics and hope

Dalits of India, 88
Daniel, book of (story of the three young Jews before Nebuchadnezzar), 131-33
Davidson, Robert, 162n
De La Torre, Miguel A., 97n
Decision and hope: Bonhoeffer and, 14-18, 27-28, 80-81; decision to be faithful to the earth for the sake of the things above, 27-28; decision to enter the politics of resistance, 16-18; decision to "stand up without compromise," 14-18; finding the place where Christ stands (and decisions are made), 16, 80-81
Defiance campaigns (1950s), 73-75, 171
DeGruchy, John W., 85-86n
DeYoung, Curtiss Paul, 11n, 41, 49n, 133n
Digger Manifesto, 30n
Discontent, hope of: Accra Confession, 51-60; CWM Assembly's "statement of discontent," 50-51, 127-28; and our obligations as God's children, 50-60, 65-66; and politician-dreamers (making

discontent the heart of their politics), 150
Dixon, Valerie Elverton, 149n
Dominion, 53-54
Dreaming and hope, 146-74; biblical story of Joseph the dreamer, 149, 152-67; hoping as dreaming, 147-52; Mandela's dream of freedom, 146, 167-73, 176; Martin Luther King's dream, 147-49; Obama's dream, 146, 147-49, 172-74; politics, dreaming, and hope (politician-dreamers), 147-50, 167-74; reconceptualizing the American dream, 149; restlessness of dreamers, 151-52, 155-56
Dunleavy, Steve, 111
Durra, Mohammed al-, 99
Dyson, Michael Eric, 128n

Ebenezer Baptist Church (Atlanta), 149
Ecological destruction, 51, 53-55; and "dominion," 53-54; Moltmann on, 54-55; standing with Mother Earth, 89; wholeness of life and "kinship" with nature, 53-54
Economic injustice and inequalities, 5-10, 51-53, 60-62; and the ANC, 5n, 8; children and poverty, 10, 61; global markets/global capitalism, 57; neoliberal globalization, 8, 52; political approaches/hopeful approaches, 139; and the "scandalous world" of the Accra Confession, 60-62; South Africa, 4, 5-10; standing with the poor and vulnerable, 88; statistics, 60-61; U.S. and Obama administration, 10-11
Elijah, 9-10, 30, 72, 82, 157
Elisha, 9-10, 82

Empire, 55-60; Accra Confession's definition, 55-60; all-encompassing reality of, 57-58; American imperialist militarism, 100-104, 106-7, 111-14, 115; colonization of consciousness, 59; consumerist gospel proclaimed through propaganda, 58-59; global markets/global capitalism, 57; idolatry and theopolitics of omnipotence, 38-39, 103, 106-7; imitation of the power of Yahweh, 9-10; imperial arrogance and myth of redemptive violence, 58; injustice and lack of compassion, 59-60; Isaiah and the Babylonian/Persian empires, 175, 176-82; Joseph the dreamer and abuse of state power (Pharaoh's political empire), 157-62, 166; Matthew's Gospel and the Roman empire, 175, 176-78; as pervasive spirit, 58; protecting politicians against the corruption of, 172-74; reality and spirit of domination, 56-57
Erasmus of Rotterdam, 94, 105, 112, 116, 121
Evangelical Reformed Church in Germany, 55
Ezzati, Majid, 11n

Faith and hope, 123-45; audacious hope, 12-13, 127, 128, 133-41; biblical story of Daniel's friends in the fiery oven, 131-33; discovering God amidst the horror of genocide, 124-27; and failures of the church, 130-31; hope, resurrection, and women, 141-45; indomitable hope, 128; Paul and, 33, 126, 151; and the "pitter-patter of little defeats," 127-33; and resurrection of Jesus Christ, 141-43

Falk, Richard A., 39n, 94-99, 102n; on just-war tradition, 107-9; on megaterrorism, 94-99, 100, 102-3
Fanon, Frantz, 94
Female/feminine: hope as, 19-20; images of God, 38-40. *See also* Women
Ferguson, John, 110
Fischer, Eugen, 93
"Freedom Charter," 3, 74-75, 171
"Freedom songs," 84-85
Fundamentalism, Christian, 106, 108n

Gandhi, Mohandas, 94, 117
Garner, Henry Highland, 8
Gender justice and equality, 108n. *See also* Women
Genocides: African, 92n, 93, 124-27; discovering God amidst the horror, 124-27; and megaterrorism, 96; and the Nazi Holocaust, 92-93, 124, 129; Rwandan, 124-27, 138n
Globalization and transnational political communities, 97-99
God with the wounded knee (Tsui// Goab), 34-38
Gourevitch, Philip, 124
Graham, Bob, 130n
The Great Terror War (Falk), 95-97
Green, Clifford J., 16n, 80n
Griffin, David Ray, 38-39n, 101n, 102n
Grotius, Hugo, 111n
Guevara, Ché, 94

Hagar, 30, 46-47, 82
Hahn, Theophilus, 35n, 37n
Hamilton, Victor P., 157n
Hannah, biblical story of (1 and 2 Samuel), 48, 73, 82, 94, 134-35
Hategekimana, Celestin, 125

Nazism, 16-18, 80-81
"Necklacing," 118-20
Neoliberal capitalism, 8, 52
Nephelim (Genesis 6), 54
9/11 terrorist attacks, 95-97, 99-105
Nonviolence: and Christian responsibility to prevent war/seek peace,
115-16, 117-23; King and, 90, 117,
121-22; South African struggle
against apartheid regime, 73-76,
117-21, 143-45, 171. See also War
and peace
Ntsikana, John, 84

Obama, Barack, 3-5, 12-13, 146,
147-49, 172-74; election as U.S.
president (2008), 3-4, 12-13,
147-49; inability to sustain a
prophetic ministry, 136-41; and
just-war tradition, 104n, 105, 114;
and King's dream, 137n, 147-49;
Nobel acceptance speech, 104n,
105, 114; political dream, 146, 147-
49, 172-74; politics and audacity
of hope, 12-13, 133, 136-41; and
politics of cynicism, 1, 4-5, 10-14;
on terrorism, 104n; and U.S.-led
war on terror, 113-14
Omar, Irfan A., 97n
Omnipotence: and idolatry, 38-39,
54-55, 103, 106-7; Keller on theology of, 38-39, 103, 106-7

Pacific Islanders, 88
Pagans, Christians as, 86-87
Palestinians, 88, 162n
Palmer, Parker J., 22-23
Pan Africanist Congress, 75
Patriarchy: children of hope and the
challenge to, 48-49; and language
of a masculine, warrior God,
38-39
Paul: on boasting ("to glory in"), 28-

29, 33; on "earth vessels" (second
letter to Corinthians), 2-3; faith
and hope, 33, 126, 151; letter to the
Romans, 69-70, 73, 83, 87, 126
Pauw, Jacques, 124n
Plaatje, Sol, 67-68, 73
Politics and hope, 1-23, 136-41,
146-52, 167-74, 175-76; "audacity"
in, 141; and audacity of hope,
136-41; blaming people's high
expectations, 11-13; Christians'
involvement in, 21-23; creating
a politics worthy of the human
spirit, 21-23; and cynicism, 1-14;
daring to speak of political hope,
2-14; election of Mandela, 3-4,
12; election of Obama, 3-4, 12-13,
147-49; making discontent the
heart of politics, 150; Mandela's
dream, 146, 167-73, 176; necessity
of tough mind and tender heart,
150; Obama's dream, 146, 147-49,
172-74; politician-dreamers, 147-
50, 167-74; protecting politicians
against the corruption of empire
and power, 172-74; Realpolitik, 8,
139-41, 151; why political realism
cannot speak the language of
hope, 139-41
Postcolonial wars, 91-93
Poverty. See Economic injustice and
inequalities
Powerless people, standing with, 89
Progressive Christianity, American,
106
Prophetic witness: and Obama's
inability to sustain a prophetic
ministry, 136-41; seeing the longing for justice of those who suffer,
63-64; seeing the world through
eyes of the poor and suffering
(three key issues), 62-65; seeing
through Jesus' eyes, 62-63; under-

South African War (1899-1902), 69
Stahl, Lesley, 104
Stephanson, Ander, 102n
Stewart, Gina M., 147n, 148
Stiglitz, Joseph, 61
Stiltner, Brian, 111n
Strijdom, J. G., 144
Struggle and hope, 41-42, 67-89; audacious hope in spite of suffering, 12-13, 127, 128, 133-41; Bonhoeffer, 80-81, 85-87; the God of the struggle for justice and liberation, 70-74; grieving with God/participation in God's suffering, 85-89; hope and the cross, 72; hope's birthplaces, 72; hope's challenge to earthly powers, 71-72; hope's emergence in encounter with suffering and struggle, 70-75; indomitable hope, 128; singing with hope, 83-85; standing in the place where Christ stands (among the suffering), 80-83, 87-89; struggles for justice/struggles in hope, 41-42. See also South African liberation struggle against apartheid regime; Woundedness and hope

Tanzania, 140n
Tennyson, Alfred Lord, 129
Ter Schegget, G. H., 152n
Terreblanche, Sampie, 5n
Terrorism, 94-105; Falk on, 94-99, 100, 102-3; genocidal character, 96; and just-war tradition, 107-8, 112-13, 116; megaterrorism, 94-99, 101, 102-3, 129; the 9/11 attacks and U.S. response, 95-97, 99-105; roots of, 93; U.S. foreign policy and "war on terror," 94-105, 107-8, 112-13, 116; view "from below," 99-105. See also War and peace
Thomas, Frank A., 10n, 149

Townes, Emilie, 141n
Trafficked women and children, 88
Trible, Phyllis, 13n
Trinity United Church of Christ (Chicago), 133
Triumphalism, Christian, 45
Tutu, Desmond, 123, 142

Ubuntu, 119, 121, 169
United Democratic Front (South Africa), 3, 118, 171
United Nations Children's Fund (UNICEF), 10
United States: criminal justice system and the "new Jim Crow," 10-11; foreign policy and "war on terror," 94-105, 107-8, 112-13, 116; imperialist militarism/empire, 100-104, 106-7, 111-14, 115; policies of preemptive war, 109, 111-14; social and economic injustice and inequalities, 10-11. See also Obama, Barack
Uniting Reformed Church in Southern Africa, 49-50, 55
Untouchables of India, 88

Van Aarde, Andries, 62
Van Selms, A., 158n, 159, 162n, 163-64
Viljoen, Stella, 108n
Villa-Vicencio, Charles, 119n
Violence. See Nonviolence; War and peace

Wallis, Jim, 142n
Walmart empire and the Walton family, 61
War and peace, 90-122, 129-30; American imperialist militarism, 100-104, 106-7, 111-14, 115; brutalizing effects of internalized violence, 117-21; Christian

responsibility to prevent war/seek peace, 105, 108-10, 114-22; colonial and postcolonial wars, 91-93; dilemma of the drawn sword, 110-14; drone warfare, 11, 113, 129; Erasmus of Rotterdam, 94, 105, 112, 116, 121; genocides, 92-93, 96, 124-27; imperial arrogance and myth of redemptive violence, 58; jihad, 96-98; justifications of war as a "lesser evil"/"lesser good," 110; just-war tradition, 92, 105-14; and language of a masculine, patriarchal, warrior God, 38-39; megaterrorism, 94-99, 101, 102-3, 129; the 9/11 attacks, 95-97, 99-105; preemptive war, 109, 111-14; targeting of civilians, 112-13; U.S. foreign policy and "war on terror," 94-105, 107-8, 112-13, 116. *See also* Terrorism

Warnock, Raphael, 147, 148, 149-50
Washington, James M., 122n
Watts, George Frederic, 134-35
Webster, Alexander F. C., 106n, 110n
Westermann, Claus, 156n, 159-60
Weussmann, Johann, 53n
"White man's burden," 100
Whitehead, Stephen M., 108n
Willimon, William H., 137, 147n, 148-49
Wilmore, Gayraud S., 8n
Wines, Michael, 100n
Wink, Walter, 57, 58, 110

Women: feminine images of God, 38-40; gender justice and equality, 108n; hope as female, 19-20; resurrection and hope, 141-45; and South African struggle against apartheid regime, 123, 143-45; trafficked, 88
Women's March on the Union Buildings of Pretoria (1956), 123, 143-45
Woodill, Joseph, 110n
World Alliance of Reformed Churches, Accra Confession of, 51-60
World Bank, 140n
World War I, 68-69, 91
World War II, 14-18, 80-81, 91, 92-93, 117
Woundedness and hope, 24-42; and alternative images of God, 34-40; exhortation of seventeenth-century slave not to "lose the glory of God," 24, 29-32; feminine images of God as mourning mother and liberator, 38-40; finding hope in woundedness/suffering, 28-34; the Khoi-Khoi God with the wounded knee, 24, 34-38, 40; Paul to the Romans (let us glory in our hope but let us also glory in our sufferings), 28-29. *See also* Struggle and hope
Wright, Jeremiah, 25, 133-36, 139

Yemen, 114, 115n

Index